Smartish Pace

Issue 30

Baltimore, Maryland

Smartish Pace

EDITOR	ASSISTANT EDITORS	INTERN
Stephen Reichert	Samuel Cheney	Nicholas Anderson
	Meg Eden	
SENIOR EDITOR	Jared Fischer	GRAPHIC DESIGNER
Daniel Todd	Kari Hawkey	Karen Siatras
	Jocelyn Heath	
ASSOCIATE EDITORS	Kristin Lindholm	COVER DESIGNER
Clare Banks	Austin Tremblay	Stephen Reichert
Daniel Cryer	Clifford Williams	
Traci O'Dea		DIRECTOR OF DEVELOPMENT
Freeman Rogers		Diane Banks

FRONT & BACK COVERS: Laura Amussen, American (b. 1973), front, *Fungi study* (red), 2022, fabric, wood, faux moss, and pearls; back, *Fungi study* (small: red), 2022, fabric, wood, and faux moss.

At the trial, before Erskine J., at the last Summer Assizes for the county of Worcester, it appeared that the plaintiff, having fettered the fore feet of an ass belonging to him, turned it into a public highway, and at the time in question the ass was grazing on the off side of the road about eight yards wide, when the defendant's wagon . . . coming . . . at what the witness termed a smartish pace, ran against the ass, knocked it down, and the wheels passing over it, it died soon after . . . .
Davies v. Mann, England, Exchequer, 1842.

Smartish Pace: Issue Thirty, April 2023. *Smartish Pace* (ISSN 1532-3218) is published by Smartish Pace, Inc., a nonprofit corporation. INDIVIDUAL SUBSCRIPTION RATES: $20.00/2 Issues, domestic & Mexico, $22.00 Canada, $24.00 elsewhere. LIBRARY/INSTITUTIONAL SUBSCRIPTION RATES: $24.00 domestic & Mexico, $26.00 Canada, $30.00 elsewhere. Subscribe online at www.smartishpace.com or send name, address, and check or money order. SUBMISSIONS: Send SASE for guidelines, or visit our website. © Copyright 2023 by Smartish Pace, Inc. All rights reserved. Copyrights to all materials published in *Smartish Pace* revert to the respective creator after publication. Printed in the United States of America. *Smartish Pace*, P.O. Box 22161, Baltimore, MD 21203 - www.smartishpace.com

Issue 30 Contents

Christopher Childers	1	Miasma
Peter Grandbois	2	Crow Considers God's absence
	3	Formula for Living Forever
Emily Lee Luan	4	Who Am I to Declare Against Your Need
	5	The Tear is Always Anything but Itself
	6	At the Acropolis Museum, We Watch
	8	窟
Sara Moore Wagner	9	When Everything Seemed Possible
	10	Ohio's Other Annie Oakley
Tanya Olson	12	Don't Come Home
	15	We the Menopausal
Christopher Kondrich	18	Rainfall on the Side of the Street
	20	The Leaf That Produces the Plant
Rae Armantrout	21	Reporting
	22	The Uncertainty Principle
	23	Powers and Dominions
	24	Words
	25	You Come Too
Fabio Pusterla translated by Will Schutt	26	To Those to Come
	27	A Quelli che Verranno
Edgar Kunz	28	Missing It
Eva Heisler	30	Strange Math, Dickinson
	32	On a Sticky Cow-Lying Summer Afternoon in 1947
Elizabeth Hazen	34	After Seshadri's "Cliffhanging"

Matt Hohner	36	To a Foster Mother
Amanda Moore	37	May Day
David Moolten	38	Apostle
Landen Raszick	39	Periphery
Jared Joseph	42	Camilla Says I Hate You to Me 7 or 8 Times at 2 Bars in 1 Night
Julie Sheehan	45	Not Here We Are
	46	The Humble Administrator's Garden
Oksana Maksymchuk	48	Coarse & Uneven Pearls
	49	Involuntary Gameness
	50	Pareidolia
Jared Harél	51	If I Never Find God
	52	Swim Lessons
	53	Survival Mode
Daniel Borzutzky	54	Sustainable Growth #205
	59	Market Volatility #311
	63	Best Practices #1015
Austin Allen	66	Conspiracy Song
Lynn Levin	67	Pharaoh's Greyhound
David Lehman	68	Landscape With Beer Can
	69	Time Travel
Rachel Hadas	70	The Melt

Maria Zoccola	71	Interlude: the Swan Describes an Invasive Species
Jesse Nathan	72	Pastoral Walking (With You) in a Field at Dawn
Kim Addonizio	73 74	Beatitude Therefore I Am Nothing
Tiphanie Yanique	76 78	The Truth About Our Family, a golden shovel "Under this tree, some of the women, who joined Queen Mary Thomas, in the rebellion of 1878, were burned alive"
Rowan Ricardo Phillips	81	Postlude
Maurice Manning	84 86 87	A Penitentiary Rocking Chair Hay-rake The Golden Treachery of Poetry
Heather Hamilton	88	But out Loud
Sylvia Jones	90 91	Generational Conflict Bob Kaufman Like Tendencies
Ned Balbo	92	Redemptions in Stained Glass
Nazifa Islam	94 95 96	How to Write Poems Bohemian Whole and Human
Hílda Davis	97	J'ouvert, 2012

Amorak Huey	98	Autumn Darling Nigh
Don Bogen	99	From the Valley Floor
Jane Lewty	104	Clairvoyant City Triptych
Felicia Zamora	107 108	To Put Meat Back Monopoly
Jessa Queyrouze	110	Teeth
Louise Ling Edwards	111	Grandmother's Eggroll Recipe
Subhaga Crystal Bacon	112	Parsing the Nonbinary
Gregory Djanikian	114 115	What Is It We Said Instructions for a Disappearance
Zebulon Huset	117 118	Universally Remote The Cutting Room Floor
Poetry Prizes	120	
Contributors	121	
Donations	127	

Christopher Childers

Miasma

The plague's a lot more boring than I thought.
I hide. I wait. I write polemic prose.
Who knows what someone has or hasn't got?

I avoid strangers, do as I was taught.
The wifi's buffering. The laptop froze.
The plague's a lot more boring than I thought.

It's in a cough, a fever, a blood-clot,
or nothing, or a swelling of the toes.
Who knows what someone has or hasn't got?

Airplanes are grounded, slots untouched. The yacht,
the sex, the stocks I wanted—it all goes.
The plague's a lot more boring than I thought.

My lying foes expose the lies I've bought.
Liars! I hope they end up comatose.
Who knows what someone has or hasn't got?

Refrigerators sputter. Bodies rot.
We slump at screens. Joints harden in the pose.
The plague's a lot more boring than I thought.

The things I used to live for, I do not.
Abstraction breeds inside me. Feeling slows.
Who knows what someone has or hasn't got?
The plague's a lot more boring than I thought.

Peter Grandbois

Crow Considers God's absence

The wind's voice stopping and starting,
wanting to speak,

unable to say anything at all

The splash of moon playing
with the lolling mist

like a homeless dog

The quiet, persistent sound of rain
like two languages

in one mouth

The trees—
everyone he's ever loved

Formula for Living Forever

Imagine you are tomorrow's rain,
or a cloud that contains
the cold calculus of seasons
ghosting over a darkening plain.
Now imagine you are the drought
at the twilit edge of things and
the world is but a veil.
Take a walk through forgetting
as minutes flood your veins.
And then it's morning again,
the mist burning away like all our emptiness
and what are you now—
a lame hawk spiraling in the distance,
crow tracks over a muddy field

Emily Lee Luan

Who Am I to Declare Against Your Need

Who am I to declare against your need
of me, mined. You and I, a likely objective.
It's easy to meet that in-between, where
the something-like-being lies. You gun
the coffee, I music the day, the heavy cloud
warbles in my chest, grows fingers for you.
What is it other than a misunderstanding—
all love, we madden towards it, outside
our webbed instincts. I wouldn't say
I know, but then again, a blue light braves
the light line; someone calls to say
call facilities. Which is to say,
the latch is fixable, time is fixed,
a long list we cross to be missed.

The Tear is Always Anything but Itself

I spend the night following leaks in the ceiling. I put
a tin can under the drip but it's too loud and keeps me
up. The night pours itself on the window screen
and the trees wave, un-astounded. I read: weeping
*is a non-coincidence with the feeling of the nearness
of terror.* I haven't wept in months.

Another night a rabbit screams a near-human scream.
The thought of a coyote hearing the sound and yet still
clawing at its beating neck—it keeps me up. The next
morning I don't want to find the severed animal
in the grass so I step gingerly, eyes to the tree line.

I twist my wrist twisting a branch off a tree—
coincidence? The leaves drip on me in great big splashes,
wetting the back of my neck. Near the tree, I can barely hear
its beating. I lean in, pour myself onto its great cracked feet.

At the Acropolis Museum, We Watch

a CGI rendering of the Venetians
blasting mortar bombs at the Parthenon;
the English chipping at the marble faces
of horses. *The reason why tourists visit America,*

my cousin says, *is to marvel that a city can be built
in a day.* He says my face is pretty, of the now.
Not like my sister, who is said to hold
an ancient kind of beauty. I find solace

and horror in the Parthenon's plundering,
its sanctity permeable—you once told me
ours was not a love that moves mountains,
romance pulled to its final unkindness.

There were years we were so at odds
with the other's moral arguments about looting
that we stopped speaking about the world
outside, satiated only by the daily walk

to the rose garden, where we wouldn't bare
our teeth at each other for love of color
and fragrance. The marble, looted
to the British museum—not the kind of burning

I found forgivable. But could I be made worth
the taking? Every evening on my way home
to you, I'd pluck the lavender that grows
at the corner of Golden Gate and Gough,

pearl the petals between my fingers.
In her anxiety to see the Parthenon, a woman

ran up the marble steps too quickly, splitting
her head at the foot of its pillars. Every evening

on my way home to you, the scent of lavender
in my palm. I knew it to be true. I would have split
myself at the foot of your love to husk it
to its facsimile. I had such a modern face for you.

I had such a modern marble face for you.

窟

Sometimes a hole sounds like cry,
a long string of o's stacked
high as an echo, with a dirt end
to the puckered lip not nearly in sigh.

Sometimes a hole sounds like cry,
the throat the hard k that round
walls bloom from.

Sometimes a hole sounds like cry—
what cradles water, what tunnels water.

Sometimes a hole sounds like cry
in this order: where the needle enters;
one who speaks for the to-be-buried;
two rising mountains.

Sometimes a hole sounds like cry,
enamored with the narrow
of its voice.

Sometimes a hole sounds like cry,
like a long postal road.

Sometimes a hole sounds like cry,
dry, dry.

Sara Moore Wagner

When Everything Seemed Possible

There's better air in Ohio,
in the space cleared to build their cabin,
wood split and polished, a shining
homestead; and they say she liked the work:
the gathering, the tending, building
the fence, the grinding down, wiping
off a counter. Mother, slender,
turns the spoon in the stew until it changes,
it's fresh tar and the road they'll name after
Annie Oakley, hands open, dirt hands,
gunpowder hands. Turns the stew into a
mirror, glossy with fat rising to the top
like glitter. What does she want beyond
this place they'll bury her—small and hand
made. They all pitch in, and she pitches in,
and the ditches are made, the coffee and rice,
boiled and poured, salted on plates. Daddy's
fresh deer hung in the shed. These are the good
days, childhood days, days written in books
with words like *work* and *whitewashed*
and *work*. Morning sunshine, morning
snow. Mourning Ohio mornings, dull
and gray, and endless.

Ohio's Other Annie Oakley

Before she was born, my mother tells me, the army
wanted to train sharpshooters, would give out free
guns and ammo and her grandfather, armed and willing to go
to war was never called, passed the tradition instead
to his granddaughters who would practice shooting
in the basement of the bowling alley.
My mother and her sisters, 1970s tall and lean, sipped
coke through straws and timed their shots to the crash
of pins and thump of the ball on the lane. Strike
for strike. My mother leaves her mother out,
leaves out her mother's body she found when she was
just fourteen, bullet ridden on the bed. My mother,
sometimes, would go upstairs to the bowling
alley, leave the guns and smoke below for
the bright lights and Jukebox where she'd play
her favorite songs: "Take Me Home, Country Roads,"
and "Fat Bottomed Girls," order crinkle cut French fries
she'd dip in chocolate milkshakes.

There was a strip mall near my childhood
home my brother and I would walk to, order fries from
the bar next to the corner store. We'd sit outside
on the curb and watch the cars pass on that big road
we weren't allowed to cross. My mother gets left out
of this story, when I tell it—maybe she was in the house,
hunched over a picture of herself with her own tired
mother. Maybe she was working at the K-mart,
or in college where she'd leave the gun smoke for good,
become a teacher—get us out, above the history
of fingers on triggers.

Annie Oakley wanted, like my grandfather,
to train girls to shoot, put them to war.

My mother, famous in her own small town
for her exacting aim never puts a gun in my hands,
tucks me in like this: the whole world is yours,
sleep, then get up. You are
what you love, she tells me.

Tanya Olson

Don't Come Home

a-drinking Miss Loretta sang
with loving on your mind
Loretta wrote that after she
and Patsy Cline became friends
Patsy taught Loretta how to move
what to say what to wear on stage
Taught her that the song not family
not love could structure her life
Told her she was the one
with the talent in that marriage
and it was time to quit taking
Doo's guff No woman knows
how to woman until she is taught
No artist is an artist unless she
pleases first herself Only let them
come home if they come home right

Patsy and Loretta's friendship
is the core of *Coal Miner's Daughter*
the rare movie made about a woman singer
The only movie I stop to watch
when I see it on TV A movie
that teaches how to be the artist
you are meant to be when nobody
says be that artist A movie that shows
the cost of art to the artist Sissy Spacek
followed Loretta around for a year
to get ready for that role Learned
how to sound like her Walk like her
Sang with her on stage at the Opry
Two Lorettas up there side by side
If you made me do a Loretta Lynn
impersonation right now I would do

Patsy's always saying 'Little girl
you got to run your own life' But
my life's running me Me doing Spacek
doing Loretta doing Patsy Such a long
lineage So many knots in the string

When Loretta had twins
she named one Peggy and one Patsy
After her sister After Cline
When we moved to Georgia the first
friend my mother made was named
Peggy and I learned to call her
Miss Peggy since she was a grownup
I knew through my parents Miss Peggy
had the slowest steepest accent ever
Tanya she would say when I saw her
around town my name tumbling
down a hill *It sure is good to see you*
You tell your momma I said Hey
One afternoon at the Food Lion
I said hello to Miss Peggy in line
only to have her turn around
and give me a one arm squeeze
Hey Sugar I'm Patsy not Peggy
Looked the same Laughed the same
Talked the same Identical twins
Just like in soap operas No two
people were ever more alike
Not Peggy and Patsy Lynn
Not Sissy Spacek and Miss Loretta
Not me and my mother

Soaps are the best because
every day is a new chapter
of the longest story most of us

ever know Characters might die
on soaps but seldom do they stay dead
Old characters return with some
cockamamie explanation A new actor
steps in and everyone pretends
they always looked just like that
Miss Loretta died the other day
The Peggys and the Patsys gone too
Beulah and Edna and Edith and Mildred
all have moved along End
of the string Last of the knots
Never a stranger to meet

We the Menopausal

have a service to offer America A timely
service only we can offer A service
we perform best You see to be menopausal
is to be porous What is meant to stay in

leaks out Pee Hair Farts Words Grunts
Groans Thoughts On sitting On standing
While walking Having access to what
others lock away is a real power For to be

menopausal is to erupt Geothermal
vent open to a fiery molten core
Cooking from the inside out how my
mother described hot flashes Menopausal

early like my mother I spend this year
trying not to die the same age
my mother died Eaten alive
as fires roiled inside her *Hot so hots*

Susan and I call them since that
is what we say as we throw off
the covers and flap the extra loose
pajamas we bought when the flames

began to bloom inside us Ceiling
fan runs Bedside fan oscillates year
round Moods swing back Swing forth
More patient than ever But also shorter

of temper For to be menopausal
is to be reversible Hot to cold Patient
to enraged No transition No clear
trigger Just the sudden flash Longer

vision Shorter fuse Depth Speed Fury
the gifts of the menopausal Together
they offer the possibility of responsible
anger A service of focused hate An ability

to bring death to those for whom death
would only be an improvement A burden
not to be hoisted by just anyone Imagine
an open fire hose left in the hands

of a child *Don't say hate You should never
hate anybody* mothers warn us as they wipe
away grade school tears In the right
hands though At the right time though Hate

becomes a tool A pressure washer designed
to strip out the deepest stains Double
jacket attack hose built to knock down
the worst fires One hand poison One hand

cure No time left to value the valueless
Now is not the time to struggle
over the mountain when we can simply
blast through instead Wedge a stick

of dynamite in any fissure Boom Only
the menopausal do it as it should be
done Who else is willing to cook
the naughty children Who else turns

into a pillar of salt rather than never
see home again Tell me who tied
to a stake laughs at the scratch
of the match It takes time to access

these tools Experience to wield them well
The menopausal are best prepared to tear
down this ramshackle house Let those of us
on fire burn the rubble to the ground

Christopher Kondrich

Rainfall on the Side of the Street

Rainfall on the side of the street streams by
in the crease the street makes before jutting up

into sidewalk. I stop to watch
the dogwood petals, small white fingernails on their way

to the storm drain, or they stop me
with how small and white they are, how much

they remind me of fingernails. Petals facing the sun.
Petals whose face is in the water, with their back

to the sun, with their back in the water
facing up. Do not tell me they are the same petal.

Do not tell me they are *not* the same petal.
They aren't the same as they were

just now or the same as they will be
once they slip off the edge of everything I see

into the sewer, its provisional darkness
below the street I never visit because I benefit from *away,*

from the systemic hiddenness of no world
but ours. Nothing else streams by

except for other petals through this one
spot my eyes fixate on. And for a moment,

there is weather, I am fraught with place, this pleat
in the asphalt, I don't know how else to tell you

except that the side I find myself always on,
which is not so much my body

as the idea of it, does not break down, nor fall
away exactly, but becomes threadbare, able to be seen

through. I see through it and call this attention
but it is also inattention to everything else.

The Leaf That Produces the Plant

If, as Sergio Stefano Tonzig wrote, *it is the leaf*
that produces the plant, and flower and stem,

sepal and stamen can be thought to originate in them,
grow out from the leaves given enough of what

anything needs to survive, then a body
is produced by the hands, and from them

comes wrist, tendon, socket, torso. The rest of us
the hands will not rest from forming and reforming

according to what they make us touch and who they let us
embrace for the last time. There is a last time

for everything. A body before it is filled
with embalming fluid is the last time it will be soft,

will give a little when we squeeze their hand
to reassure ourselves. I assure you

that when you look your own hands in the face,
head on, when you hold their gaze, hold

the gaze of your hands and not drop it, you will be
undone, untethered, you will not recognize who you are

because this whole time your hands have been
the source of you, your principal part

and you cannot think of yourself as mere appendage.

Rae Armantrout

Reporting

Yellow racing stripe
on the single snail
on a hot sidewalk
this morning.

*

"Experience the weather
before it happens!"

shouts the weather guy
in the fake rain.

You just go on your tone.

*

"Diesel keeps things
simple."

I heard that today
in what passes
for the void.

The Uncertainty Principle

   1

An atom "is localized
by an interaction"

the way you surprise yourself
by expressing an opinion

when asked,

one you didn't know you had
and may not hold

for long.

   2

A subatomic particle is not
its mass or spin

the way a person
is not a body

and a poem is not
what it says.

Powers and Dominions

   1

Gabriel was the announcer;
Michael made war.

The rest were hazy
                      depth of field,

sheer plenary
status—

a peasants' version
of the aristocracy

reflected across the so-called
heavens.

   2

I love my granddaughters just
as they love

Elsa and Anna
in *Frozen*.

We're discovering our powers
for the first time

in somebody's
refracted future.

Words

   1

Most thought is trash talk.
Stop!

When I sit quietly,
I feel like I'm waiting

for words
to break time up,

pulsate.

   2

I might think of something
and not have its name.

Then it comes—
special delivery.

Who was tasked
with finding it?

Where would she be
without this work?

You Come Too

What I like best
is a reflection,

a vestige:

faint white
Xmas tree lights

hovering outside
the window pane
at dawn,

an afterlife's
afterlife—

like a poet's poet—

as if without moving
we could go on
and on

Fabio Pusterla *translated by* Will Schutt

To Those to Come

meaning you, who'll turn back
and look at us from the peaks
of your brilliant age, like one who scans a valley
he can't recall having crossed:
you won't see us behind the screen of fog.
But we were here, ministering to the voice.
Not every day, not every hour
of the day, only from time to time,
when mustering a little strength
appeared possible.
We'd close the door
behind us, abandoning
our sumptuous homes,
and, picking up the path again, drift on.

A Quelli che Verranno

Allora voi, che volgerete
lo sguardo verso di noi dalle vette
dei vostri tempi splendidi, come chi scruta una valle
che non ricorda neppure di avere percorsa:
non ci vedrete, dietro lo schermo di nebbie.
Ma eravamo qui, a custodire la voce.
Non ogni giorno e non in ogni ora
del giorno; qualche volta, soltanto,
quando sembrava possibile
raccogliere un po' di forza.
Ci chiudevamo la porta
dietro le spalle, abbandonando
le nostre case sontuose
e riprendevamo il cammino, senza meta.

Edgar Kunz

Missing It

It's a new life: the tidy
brick bowfront joined

to its neighbors, the long
yard clotted with ivy

and vasevine we tore out
and burned in a heap,

edge of her shovel turning up
a Twix wrapper, shards

of brick, a marble made of hot
pink plastic. We miss

our old city, we say: the
poppies bushing up

at the light posts, throwing
the windows wide to let in

the cold, the high
electric whistling

of the rails—and the light,
we say, god, the light

most of all. We miss it,
we say, hammering

garden boxes together
from a friend's trashed fence.

The light—as we plant squashes
and peas, and give them

a trellis to climb.

Eva Heisler

Strange Math, Dickinson

I read the dash as a minus sign.

"Sea" minus "More Seas" equals "Desert."

~

Clock minus "Prospect's half" equals the "o" of "halo."

~

Each vowel is a buttonhole.
I practice

the buttonhole stitch.

Make one loop over the edge.
Gently pull the thread to secure the knot.

~

"Trees" minus "distant Light" equals "Traveller on a Hill."

~

I am that elderly woman buttoning her coat.
Her hands tremble, and each button
is like a stone she's trying
to push through wool.

~

"Health" minus "Safety, and the Sky" equals "Exile."

~

As if the Sea should part / And show a further Sea—

As if the calendar should part / And show a further calendar—

~

To find the blue region, first find the big square
and then subtract the little square.

On a Sticky Cow-Lying Summer Afternoon in 1947

The child was carted off in a hay wagon,
still carrying the soldier doll,

pinking shears hidden in a pocket.
Banished to Broken Oak Road

where someone's grandmother
was to school her in what's what.

The air was wadding-thick,
sticky like flypaper. Thunder coming.

From her pocket, the child pulled a sandwich
and her aunt's new Wiss Pink-Rite scissors,

the blades like pitched roofs—
a village of houses razor-sharp

and threatening to pink the sky.
She tried them out,

pinking the wax paper
in which her bologna sandwich was wrapped,

pinking an oily rag in the wagon,
pinking the soldier doll's felt pants,

pinking the top of her socks.
She was headed for trouble

but what they would never find:
the jigsaw puzzle piece in her left shoe.

She could hear her mother
ordering the sisters to look under the sofa,

between the cushions, in the candy jar
for the last piece of the puzzle,

and it pleased the child
her family would never complete

the picture of a windmill in moonlight,
that there would be a hole in the moon,

and the missing piece was in her shoe.

Elizabeth Hazen

After Seshadri's "Cliffhanging"

> *I won't let myself fall, but I don't want to pull myself up.*
> *I'm ambivalent. I'm ambivalent forever now.*
> *But if you were here, looking down on me and saying,*
> *"Grab my hand, grab my hand," I would, I know, I surely would.*
> —from "Cliffhanging" by Vijay Seshadri

This morning you told me you don't care
about feeling better anymore: you've adapted
to the nagging doom, the dirt we brush beneath
the carpet, the other shoe that always drops.
I'd say you're too young to be so dark, but
when I was your age, sadness and rage were mixed up
in everything I felt, vibrations holding me together.
You see my inconsistencies. I embrace my despair
as an old friend, even as I insist you must *fill your own cup;*
I won't let myself fall, but I don't want to pull myself up.

I've tried to hide my uncertainty, but you winced
when I said the best years are ahead, so now
I say time and age teach you to fall a little less
painfully. I say skin thins as you get older, so steel
yourself against disappointments now, practice breathing,
learn your limits, trust discriminately, don't allow
your inner critic to stifle every effort. I know it's hard,
but some days just going through the motions
is its own accomplishment; I'm still learning how.
I'm ambivalent. I'm ambivalent forever now

about everything except endorphins and rising
seas and time moving in one direction, with
or without us. It's not an easy moment to be alive.
You hear me shout at other drivers, curse my rivals,
declare I can't do it anymore. I don't know

whether everyone feels this way—that staying
in one place will do them in. I've fallen apart
before your eyes, madwoman on her knees.
I've failed to model gratitude, patience, praying—
but if you were here, looking down on me and saying,

I don't believe in anything either, I'd force myself
to stand. I'd show you, tattooed on my arm:
There are millions of suns left. Some days this optimism
is more grimace than smile, but still—I've papered
my office with verses I love, photographs of people
I love, a stack of books—the armor of my adulthood.
It's easy to turn bitter, to ignore the miraculous beating heart,
the sun's bold assertions. But if you fell, I'd call out,
Get up, keep going (I have a whole arsenal of good),
Grab my hand, grab my hand. I would, I know, I surely would.

Matt Hohner

To a Foster Mother

> *—Baltimore County Department of Social Services*
> *Location Unknown*

A half century has turned since you held me,
stared into these eyes with a charity reserved
in the knowledge I was wanted by a hopeful
couple whose love was my destination after a
gauntlet of bureaucracy and paperwork, social
workers' visits and record checks, interviews
and stamps and signatures, the bang of a
judge's gavel closing the door behind me.
But in that brief dreamtime between birth,
the giving up, and the going home, I was
yours, fed, cleaned, swaddled, and held close,
your breath and heartbeat my wind and drum,
your voice like birdsong on a short hilltop
stopover on my early migration from limbo
to life. I was too young to know your scent
now, though I must have enthralled in you
each day as you spent time with me, that most
precious human gift. Had you known that I
would squirm and cry in discomfort against
the chest of the woman whose hands received
me—awkward intuition—that she would leave
the family that became mine a decade later, you
might have held me a moment longer, hummed
one last measure of the song ending between us,
given me one final, lingering, selfless gaze
from eyes of kindness I cannot remember.

Amanda Moore

May Day

Help me decide how to celebrate: dance
or destruction. Across town, people in masks
are kicking in windows, torching trash cans,
while at my daughter's school the teachers are raising
a maypole strung with candy-colored ribbon.
The truth is both feel about right: I'm angry
all the time these days,
                       and it's also finally spring.
Heat builds in the bloom-scented morning.
Our rent is paid and we are lucky. Bean sprouts crown
in rich, rested earth. Not everyone earns enough to eat. Children
garlanded in daffodils are ready to revel. Protestors, too—
clotting a street blaring with siren. It's all one,
this world: its broken machines, its warm desires.

David Moolten

Apostle

A crowd watches a drunk movie star get saved
from the Hudson. I hear groans
from the capsized Maserati as it sinks
like I'm standing there,
I've recounted this enough, more anecdote
than parable, though I leave out that it's not mine,
like your recipe for peach brandy martinis
I still pour. I have faith people will love them
even if your love turned out
to be a joke, like all the good ones,
meant to be stolen. Guy walks into a bar
and meets God instead of strangers
he feels obliged to impress,
a delusion in other words. It might have been
Clooney or Cruise or Rollo the clown,
enough when I'm drowning
someone goes in the water, they needn't walk on it.
I still stare at your wilting
poster of a late Picasso dove. I'm still drawn
to your fragrance, your blue Armani shirts
on anyone. You're neither holy nor brave,
your face luminous but barely, just in my head
like lighting a match in a cathedral,
not funny though it almost makes me smile.

Landen Raszick

Periphery

No, I don't want to go for endless tea.
I'm getting a burrito and some beer.
You don't really want to be with me.
I'm going to write a poem about the war.

None here are being killed by mortar shells,
RPGs or thermobaric bombs.
We sleep away our problems, suffer spells
of weak depression, drink and call our moms

and hear about how she received a coupon
for Blue Ribbon, a meal-kit delivery service,
how she burned a brand-new granite pan
but liked the shrimp's cilantro garlic sauce.

I say I'm also worried about Moldova,
that this is far from finished, though I hate to
pretend that anyone's guess is good. Moreover,
remember Trump wanting to exit NATO?

I still maintain he was a Russian agent
but Dave just laughs. Then he gets serious:
"It's very clear what this war is really about:
huge reserves of oil and natural gas.

America can't go to war with Russia.
In fact, this has been happening for years:
the annexations of Chechnya, Crimea.
For all the Western World's swords of words—

sanctions sanctions sanctions—they still agree
to purchase oil, to buy oil in the future,

then bury deals in talk of energy."
Dave is right about everything, I'm sure,

except he doesn't seem to credit the notion
that we could suffer a similar suffering.
Dave and mom ask if I'll play Dominion.
All my friends are playing Elden Ring,

immersed in realms of timeless tarnished souls.
I am not. I compulsively check my phone.
I don't receive a text or any calls.
The hardest part of this: I am alone.

My loneliness is absolutely abhorrent.
I have a home. I have a place to go.
I've bought a piano. I'm able to pay my rent.
I'm furious at the size of my burrito.

And so we live, swiping away on apps,
going on bad dates or hooking up,
passing easy or struggling to give a crap,
writing good poems, also poems that suck.

We watch a TikTok of a silly cat.
We aren't sure what awful news is good for.
We watch a bunny chase a wild rabbit.
We suck. We fuck. We keep watching the war.

The media pretend not to love the ratings.
The influencers forget what they called false.
My dad is still invested in his ranting
about Joe Biden, immigrants, and gas.

I am cooking pasta with ground beef.
My Hindu friends would look at me with horror.

It was cheap. I didn't see the death.
Sometimes I forget about the war.

I look out the window and see the brick façade
of my neighborhood. People are inside.
They watch TV. Most of them are good.
They pray. Some of them believe in God.

Through glass, I see a person folding laundry.
One apartment like a nightclub pulses
purple, red, blue, and green. It's lovely,
humans feeling safe from outside forces.

To think that something small as an atom splitting
could turn us all to dust. And tell me how
the only thought I have from where I'm sitting
is I love you. I wish you were with me now.

Jared Joseph

Camilla Says I Hate You to Me 7 or 8 Times at 2 Bars in 1 Night

i feel bad for not wanting to go to the beach
or go to Joshua Tree or do really anything
with Sarah so i go to the bar to do anything
with Sarah. It is her bar she is the bar
manager she's stringing up electric lights to make it her
own. There is a huge outdoor patio i sit on
a chair she sits on a chair and Camilla
falls off the chair she arrives on or
to. She is already wildly drunk and we aren't
sure why, but we are sure how. It was from
drinking. A man on a cell phone helps
her before anyone else helps her and i wonder
why i and Sarah are belonging to anyone else
's category. But we are. And so then this is
what happens. The man on the cell phone says
the chair is unstable anyway and Camilla
repeats this several times that she is not drunk
but the chair is drunk and the chair has been
drinking and the piano's been drinking and the man
said the chair
is unstable and where this man's authority comes
in, we don't know. We all joke that he is the chair
of some chair company, Camilla says he is
the Chairmaster. Camilla has a dog named
Master. i think that that's an amazing name
for a dog or chair. Sarah guesses her password.
This is an amazing moment. Camilla is
snorting laughing but also like she'll cry
with happiness. Her and all
of her friends' and Sarah's friends' Instagrams
have been recently hacked, and Camilla says it's not
the followers. It's not the followers i care about it is

not that i am beautiful that i am targeted
don't get me wrong, i'm not saying i am
gorgeous, and i don't know if i am
supposed to say she is, now, gorgeous, because she is
saying that, actually, and it appears my role is
to say that, too, though it's true Camilla
is beautiful. Is this a trap. It's not that Camilla
says. I'm a person that likes
memories. And my trips and my memories
of my trips. And now they've all gone
and been deleted by this hacker. And she keeps
yelling her password, which is
not WHATTHEFUCKdoyouknow1989
or 88, with some other special
characters, but what the fuck do i know, daring hackers
to wipe away her memory and her trips, and it's not
brazen, not actually. And now i will remember
this moment. There is only this torn
open flower on the earth. We go to Walts bar
there are some pinball machines there who
cares, and i miss Anna. i miss Anna
all night, all nights. She was a big breakup
Sarah says, huh, in the car. No one is
a breakup, i don't say. There are many moments
i don't say what i'm thinking. It is called my life.
Camilla sits on the railing and holds
court: in Russia the first time i went horseback
riding, in Russia the handler is always African
American. i don't correct her on the African
American part, although she says it many times, it isn't
salient. It is a fetishization that is sad.
i fetishize my own language skill as if
it means anything. Although language itself is
what means anything. Though there are limits.
The breeze coils around my temples like hair.

The wind winds around moving strands that i
can't see. Sarah whispers to me
about Camilla. i have been alive
before. i have been offered i
phones on IG, how they
hack you. And then Camilla invites us to go and
hatchet-throw. All you need is a little bit of anger
she says, and a lot of hope, i say. Yes, Camilla
says. Just imagine the face of someone
you hate she says. It's bullseye every time.

Julie Sheehan

Not Here We Are

Not here and never on time, the flight from SUX
(it rhymes with "sucks") connects, allegedly,
to other elsewheres that can only be
accessed from Chicago. Here's the crux

of time: it begs the fact of geography.
I ask you, like the flight from Egypt (bad)
landing the Jews in Sinai (also bad),
how elsewhere can I ever really be?

Missouri River stink, the retch of hogs
I rinse away in basins, but the flat A
when I say "bagel" no moist towelette can purge.

Like a blowdart, I hurtle toward O'Hare,
though the only motion from Seat 20-A
is pen touching down on pad. Not here we are.

The Humble Administrator's Garden

—built c. 1509, Suzhou, China

It is my wish for fleeing happiness to build a house and plant trees and to lead a free and happy existence of idleness; let there be a pond to fish from ... that is how a humble person administers his domain.
— Pan Yue, "Rhapsody on the Idle Life"

Of course it cost a fortune.
The Hall of Distant Fragrances could waft
those lotus blossoms

only after cheap labor
dug the lake and lugged the ton of water
and cultivated

inch by inch even the stones,
for rocks are no mere rocks, but scholar rocks,
curated and posed.

Let us wait in the Watching
the Pines and Appreciating Paintings
Hall—need I say more?—

at the Master of the Nets
until grunts complete the effortlessness
we fully expect.

Leaning on the Jade in spring
ought to dispel any vestige of humility
that administering

such beauty left its patron,
whose view "borrows" a pagoda. Perhaps
our host moved mountains,

or, rather, his workmen did.
Oh, look! A rustic hut some fisherman
never used, his boat

built of stone. He's out
all night in search of koi, an ornamental fish
that can't be stomached.

Oksana Maksymchuk

Coarse & Uneven Pearls

Don't instruct me to craft
sentences clean as bone

Instead, let me present
with a baroque stroke

searching and curvilinear
encrusting each whorl

with a jagged gem

the calm of clams
siphoning water

they are submerged in
as it—slowly—comes to

a rolling boil
until they open

Involuntary Gameness

The nerve of trees lining
the rocky slopes!

Of bombes devoured
in bombed-out cities!

Of flowers, of birds
their contours more vibrant now
against the wreckage

Of children's voices—
a joyful taut cannonade—
rushing in through the windows

shattered by a blast wave

Pareidolia

I could be silent now
locked up in a cellar
minding the business of survival
intimate & immediate

And yet, here I am, inside
a song like inside another's
slashed-open gut
keeping warm

in the darkness that falls
billowing out
like an inkblot, an angry
talking cloud

Jared Harél

If I Never Find God

—for and after Baruch & Yehoshua November

it may be because I search
like how my daughter dawdles
about our modest two-bedroom:

dreamy, off-kilter, driving
me mad, too lucky to really look
for her elusive other shoe.

Swim Lessons

To save them from drowning,
we let our children sink
into the arms of an instructor
in the old basement pool
of our local JCC. Once a week
for forty-five minutes, my wife and I
watch on white plastic chairs
as they practice not dying
with mixed results. One lesson
they learn their bodies must
be violent to stay afloat.
Next lesson, to stay afloat,
they must be perfectly still.
But mostly it's a rash of erratic
splashes. They blow bubbles
and kick in pink and blue
swim caps. Reptilian goggles
press circles into their skin.
Later when they emerge
chlorine-slick and shivering
above the teal tiled floor,
we wrap them up and swear
how brilliant they were,
which is the lie we gift ourselves
before pulling them in.

Survival Mode

Our daughter is killing villagers again.
I'm upset because we'd talked about this—
the villager killing—last week over dinner,
and how we're totally not okay with it.
Now here she is, killing villagers again.
It was different this time, our daughter insists,
I just needed somewhere to sleep. She spears
a single green bean, lifts it to her lips.
*You can't get mad at me for needing somewhere
to sleep!* Our son nods along, either listening
or bouncing his bangs into his eyes.
My wife and I glance at each other.
Truth be told, we need more information.
What was she doing roaming a village
with nowhere to sleep? Was killing really
the last reasonable resort? Couldn't
she have bartered, or built her own bed?
We're set to interrogate when our son
suddenly stops bobbing his head to ask
what a villager looks like dead. *Oh,*
says our daughter, setting down her fork.
*You know how dead cows look? All red after they fall
to the ground? Same with villagers. They just die
and that's it. And then they disappear.*

Daniel Borzutzky

Sustainable Growth #205

What what what what   what do you cost

What what what what   what do you cost

How much how much how much   how much are they willing to give you

How much how much how much   how much are they willing to give you

What will you give them
What will you give them
What will you give them
What will you give

I will give them my face

    I need six dollars

I will give them my hand

    I need five dollars

My mouth is dead

I will give them something from my mouth

My mouth is dead

I need twenty-seven dollars for rice eggs bread milk

I'll sell my meta-data for twenty-seven dollars

I'll sell you the meta-data in the meta-data of my meta-data

What does my face cost?

    I need seven dollars for lunch

Meta-data says I bought too many books about mental illness

    What?

What does my condition cost?

I need to assess the meta-data on my skin

How much for these knuckles?

How much for these ankles?

I will give them thirty-four hours a week   I will give them fifty-two hours a week   I will give them 212 hours a month   I will give them twelve hours a day   I will give them eight   forty-three   fifteen

Shhhhhh   Shhhhhh   Don't need to go to a third party for my meta-data I'll sell you my password   (Hr8491$what)

They test my meta-data for toxicity

I have too many assets in my portfolio   but I don't own any of them

The assets are bloody

The assets are untimely

The assets are drowning

I look for my body but it's under water
I look for my meta-data but it's under water
I look for my value but it's tied up in the meta-data in my meta-data

I look for my time but they tell me it's just a metaphor

I cannot interpret the metaphor unless I pay forty-six dollars

    So many names for what I owe

Is your face really a surveillance machine that can hijack refugee data?

    So many things to put in my mouth

I have wrapped my head in double-grade fabric designed to block signal detection

    So many openings to fill with blank verse

    So many holes

    So many overpriced metaphors

I don't know where they put my body

Need less contaminated data need more unwavering data need more robust data

Need to get the dead kids out of my data

I need six dollars for lunch

I need two dollars for the bus

I need five dollars to make it through the purge today

I cost more than I used to cost and less than my neighbors cost

I need a more precise assessment of my social relations

My exchange value needs to be corroborated

I need to know the most profitable body part to invest in

My house is underwater

I need to find the bridge

The bridge the boat the dollar the mouth the money the weather

The judge says the state won't return my data or my meta-data until I can prove it won't be used for criminal activity

The value of my data is 400 dollars

I already paid 900 dollars in court fees and still I can't get my data back

I meet with a lawyer who says he can help me get my data back

We'll need some ripe organs   he says

I only have one decent kidney

What about antibodies?

The royalties on my antibodies were only thirty-seven dollars last year

He helps me unload some algorithms and I ask the judge to return my data baby

Judge says   you'll need to rehumanize your face before I let you
          touch that stuff again

I go back to the bank

They say my face can be exchanged for the future meta-data of
          poor kids in developing countries who will soon be middle
          class

A banker tests my body for redundancies

He sends me to the vault for an appraisal

They take my DNA and I sign some papers I don't understand and
the data analyst congratulates me

You are lucky   she says

You will always be human again

Market Volatility #311

A conglomerate of investors in New York   Shanghai   London   Frankfurt   Tokyo and Sao Paulo own the cache of kidneys

I should really look away from the two men yelling at each other   but I'm too curious about what might happen next

We wait for the fifty day moving average of the kidney's price action to drop beneath the line of resistance

Is this the right time to buy?

My father says   I see you there son   your leg is swelling   that might be a symptom of too much protein in your urine

The price movement is unnatural   the bears are attacking the bulls   a bull says   at least I don't spend my life hoping that other people will suffer   that individual investors will lose all their money   that businesses will fail and go bankrupt

The bull follows this up with a meme of a big grizzly bear sodomizing a smaller one

At home   nervous consumers on their phones and computers ask   is this the right time to invest in a hangover elixir made from CBD?

My doctor would be a better doctor if he wasn't such an asshole

Outside my window a man yells I only have one bullet what the hell am I supposed to do with just one bullet?

All my life I've had an astigmatism   I don't know what that actually means

The price of the kidneys is about to skyrocket   still the buyers don't feel safe enough to invest

She says   *your work sounds unrealistic*   but everything I write is something I've experienced in quote-un-quote real life

The immune system can both attack the body and be attacked by the body

Is this a good time to search for a hollowed-out space in which to hide from the world forever?

The only thing he remembers about the short story is how all the tourists go blind when they look up at the sky during the eclipse

Fascism and progress go hand in hand   is that your chocolate in my peanut butter?

I want to believe the tele-doctor is deeply studying my face so I move my cheek up against the computer screen and ask her if she has enough light

Certain words sound great in one language and terrible in another   I sound stupid when I express anger and frustration in French

The tour guide says   don't worry   nothing will

happen if you look at the sun   the tourists don't know he's a member of Opus Dei who tortures young communists in his basement

It's natural to prefer artificial intelligence to natural intelligence   he says   as he presses his lips to his cell phone

He thinks he can say just about anything in a poem if he says it in the right tone of voice

You can pay money to simulate a deadly border crossing through the desert

You can pretend you are dehydrating   you can collapse or weep uncontrollably or drape yourself over the bodies of strangers and ask them to drag you for miles

She asks me if I want to start a Meetup for people who like bowling and who also want to destroy the entire structure of the nation-state

A good way to write a poem is by taking several other poems you have written and combining them so that the poem has multiple themes and timeframes.

She says   some people want to go bowling   others want to destroy the nation-state   some people want to go bowling *and* destroy the nation-state

I didn't hear what you said   I was too busy looking at my phone.

If you are patient you can make money by just sitting there doing nothing

The economist wonders   should I design a country with a healthcare system controlled and regulated by the government   or should people take their chances on the free market where supply and demand and the coercive laws of competition dictate how we receive our health care?

I only write about death and suffering   she's surprised to learn I'm cheerful

In the Q and A an audience member asks   is there room in your writing for joy?

It's a terrible question and I don't want to answer it but she's the only person who raises her hand and somewhere in my heart I feel grateful

I don't care that much about freedom   I just don't want to be trapped here anymore

The poster in the doctor's office reads   *Health: The Only Wealth that Matters*

What's the difference between my husband and this chair

This chair doesn't mind if I piss on it

Best Practices #1015

She pulls out her passport and the agent says   your country no longer exists

We tread lightly over the broken bones so we won't cause them to explode or decay

He wants to know the name of this atrocity so he can classify it among the previous ones

We dig deeper into our faces to find the acceptable calculations that might alter the course of history   (is it too soon to embellish the dead?)

Time passes   Nothing changes   The hours become worse and worse

There is a militarized frontier in your face and you cover it with the sixty-four digit code that all the miners are searching for

We can't advance until we know the name of this period of infinite gestation

They need to build a system whose death leads to the most efficient form of regeneration

We rebuild the means of production and when we run out of resources we call the toll free hotline and ask for a resumption of the oppressive policies that have destroyed us for so many centuries

I'm so tired I could sleep on a barbed wire fence   is not a sentence you want to say in certain contexts

I'm sorry you think my body reminds you of a South American vortex whose name you can't pronounce

If the city would explode a bit more politely then we might be able to attract the sorts of entrepreneurs who can finance the futurity of our misery

I mean   what is the first thing you think of when you encounter the spiritual transgression of your body in a tunnel between the absence of time and the hypercirculation of capital?

There's a name for this experience   but I'm not allowed to mention it

The child barking in the tree signals to his neighbors that the tourists are coming with their guns again

The game ends when they recolonize the natives and force them to speak to the wrong god in the wrong language

The new hemisphere appears on the horizon   no one is there to authenticate it

What nation-state controls the sun and the moon? Which hedge fund owns this water?

We are in the future now but time keeps glitching and the earth keeps quaking backwards

You've said this before   *this kidney does not have an owner*

When the war ends they will refine and perfect all that they learned by accident

The most effective ways of reducing the population will become best practices taught at schools throughout the nation

The system requires the authentication of the sacred body that will never appear

The disappeared body is sanctified and soon the tourists will pay to see a non-fungible replication of it

The rehumanization of the population repeats itself first as parody then as encryption

Did you hear the one about the metaphor that was a metaphor for a metaphor that exists outside thought and language?

He wanted to kill some time but instead he killed the villagers

Tough break

In the future   with proper guidance   he'll surely make better decisions

The Greeks and Romans had a name for this

The foot that despises its slipper

Austin Allen

Conspiracy Song

Open your eyes, connect the dots,
ignore the alleged astronauts:
the moon is a stage and its wired-up skies
transmit the beautiful mainstream lies.

Ignore the alleged astronauts;
the Feds, whose swarming nanobots
transmit the beautiful mainstream lies
jammed in our veins; and the Vatican spies.

The Feds (whose swarming nanobots
propagate when we get those shots
jammed in our veins) and the Vatican spies
suppress the gospel we'd otherwise

propagate. When we get those shots
color-enhanced, the truth your thoughts
suppress—the gospel we'd otherwise
preach underground—will proudly rise

and fasten all threads, resolve all plots
in the heaven of unconnected dots.
The moon is a stage and its wired-up skies
need you, need you, to open your eyes.

Lynn Levin

Pharaoh's Greyhound

Pharaoh's Greyhound, always fleet, reached
death before her master.
No more to see, grieved the king,
his racer harrowing the air
to stroke the scabbard of her snout.
Who else could approach without cowering,
almost as an equal, the crook and the flail
or fathom the frets of the mighty?

Pharaoh imagined the dog whimpering in abandonment
unable to understand the why of suffering and death.
Too much to bear, he thought, watching
his morticians draw out the dog's organs

and drop them into canopic jars.
For nights the king dreamed
of having himself killed,
of begging his palace guards to do him in.
Oh, to be with the beloved companion
both bandaged against the wound of death,
there to console each other in the musty tomb.
The dog faithful, the king faithful
together on the dark shore.

David Lehman

Landscape With Beer Can

—for Terence Winch

The language of politics is the enemy
of the language of poetry. And the alternative
to political poems is not limited to poems
about flowers (though Wordsworth's
host of daffodils give me a lift in March)
and trees (Frost's "Birches" in the fall),
but you can put in all sorts of things,
including the Rolling Rock beer can
on the side of the frozen brook, the blue
of the sky with a white stripe across it,
the bubbles at the base of the falls,
the outline of the pines and birches
when winter's opinions prevail,
and snow covers the earth.

Time Travel

I am not wounded in my dreams.
No, I walk freely among the ruins
visiting old girlfriends
their urgent mothers
and disapproving fathers,
and as a result of my travels,
I can tell you this:
the main thing to remember is
the past and future do not exist;
you can walk up and down years
from 1972 to 2001 and the people are
the same, the décor completely different
like the 1940s kitchen we lived in
in the 1960s.

Rachel Hadas

The Melt

Dreams used to loom freighted with urgent meaning,
even if the meaning melted before morning.

What dawns have lost in their prophetic aura
they've gained in the radiance of promise.

Each new day, each dream now out of reach
beats like a heart,

adds to the length of days already lived,
subtracts from the days that remain.

We forget the images, retain
the meaning; let the meaning slip, but hold

to bird, beloved, maze, till that too slides
into the wet and melt and shine of spring.

Maria Zoccola

Interlude: the Swan Describes an Invasive Species

several methods are used to cull an unwanted swan population. shotguns, primarily, for the ease of it, for the fun of it, the harsh joy of sighting down the barrel and taking us where we float, our necks arced to our mates, our kingdom of weeds below us. kinder cullers addle our eggs, dipping them whole into corn oil to smother the porous shells, robbing the embryos of oxygen, failing them in gentle smother. still others set dogs on our young, kick over our nests, poison us with tainted feed. america killed her trumpeter swans, but she doesn't love us, her mute replacements: so beautiful, so hungry, so vehement in defending ourselves. helen, i see you. hatched from an egg, paddling ever since. born in a land that doubts your claim to it.

Jesse Nathan

Pastoral

  The anvil cloud, trundling away.
The smashed wet wheat, like a cat
  ambushed by a bath. The baby
birds strewn about. I step in what
      seems like a redwing
        under the swing—
     ants scramble out.

Walking (With You) in a Field at Dawn

They sashay, those tendrils of mist.
Sunlight glitters in the wet spiderwebs
draped all over the witches' broom
flaring from the base of the tree.

Hackberry, I think. Witches' broom
a flag of panic, a casting madly outward
under the stress of something
we can't see. The tree, the only one out here

and whatever secret fears it has, the swallows
still call its upper branches home.

Kim Addonizio

Beatitude

Oh lord, I don't call anyone Lord.
I believe in the lower-case word,

the tiny multicolored lights strung
over the bar, blinking all year, the hunger

assuaged by peanuts & pork skins,
the benevolent screens of televisions

wavering benedictions
over the convivial, afflicted men,

the woman crowned with a knit hat,
all in the tempered pall of daylight—

dimlight, darklight, the lost & half-assed
more denizens than citizens who cast

their prayers high into sagging nets
tangled with lacy fish, blessed

by no one & buoyed
toward the heaven of the ceiling tiles.

Therefore I Am Nothing

It's probably best not to think too much about my terminally ill cat
or to wonder whether my mentally ill brother is dead or alive right now
which makes me think of my cat again because of Schrodinger's
      experiment—

what was it anyway—some kind of thought experiment
I remember there was a cat in a box & some poison
But I don't want to think about poison, another bad thing in my head

except that now I am, but at least I don't personally know anyone who
      was poisoned—
ancient kings & nobles, Hercules & hatters, some enemies of Putin—
so I'm feeling okay now, *poison poison poison*, no anxiety at all

People are waiting in line in Mexico to fill tanks with oxygen for dying
      abuelas
The Greenland ice sheet is melting faster than a butter stick in a
      microwave
Australian clownfish can't find the reef, all that noise from humans &
      their machines

That's how I think of it, *humans & their machines*, like I'm not one of them
But I am & now I have to bring up Descartes
who thought animals had no minds, just mechanical sensations

One more anthropocentrist ruining the picnic for everyone
Can't we all just take off our tacky outfits & be nectar in a bee-loud
      glade
Open the box, don't open the box, ignore the box, the cat knows

Also I don't understand Cartesian dualism but I hate it
with a simplistic, uncomprehending hatred
unlike the jaded & cosmopolitan disgust I feel for God

I guess the cat can't know anything if it's already dead
& something went wrong with my brother's brain years ago
& if the earth is having any thoughts they're probably along the lines of
> *Stop poisoning me*

Now I'm wondering whose ashes were scraped from the columbarium
       along with my mother's
I don't think she's playing tennis with Jesus in heaven
Mostly I try not to think at all anymore

just stare at the place between words & their meanings
& wait for some less monstrous feeling to be born
& limp toward me

Tiphanie Yanique

The Truth About Our Family, a golden shovel

The women in my family are born with legs of fin, tails for swimming
    up or pulling under.

There is one boy per generation, and so mothers are rooted to the land
    like this.
Our tails are for hunting in the sea, our boys for foraging from mango
    and any bearing tree.

We speak in tongues: English for all, Spanish and Danish for most,
    Arawak for some.
We chose the land and were of the sea, and in this way were kin to all
    we were part of.

We learned that the ocean was earth's soul; to be born from soul made
    us made us simply the.
Though genealogy shows that for more than a hundred years, we were
    a family mostly of women.

From motherhood we learn love as a giving, then self-love as with
    sisters, before the men joined.
In our adolescence we each take a vow of lofty service, become class
    president or pageant queen.

We seek what is above us. We pray as a family. Read the pillars
    of the Bible, recite the Hail Mary.
We are no more divine than anyone, though we seek a holy life, living
    off the land of Saint Thomas.

Most of us hold onto the tradition of swimming, though we walk
    and never dive in.
Some of us take to dancing, or pan playing rather than to water. A
    form of teen rebellion.

Still, we participate in history. We loved the governor so he might
    grant freedom in the uprising of
1848. A generation later, instead of children, we carried cutlass
    and flame for the fight of 1878.

It's true, there were years when we loved men and the land so much we
    forget who we were.
But new women were born again and again, whose hope for each other
    and for the sea still burned.

Our ocean is an organic archive. Like coral, its buried things give
    home to life, its dead stories alive.

    —With gratitude to the St. Croix Historic Preservation Committee,
    who placed the plaque under the baobab tree in Frederiksted.

"Under this tree, some of the women, who joined Queen Mary Thomas, in the rebellion of 1878, were burned alive"

—a found poem, after La Vaughn Belle and Hadiya Sewer

The tree and I have something in common.
We carry archives
we are of nature.
This is a true
story.
This is not the objective
truth.
Did the individuals who created
the archive
lie or did nature make
a mistake? Who even asks
such questions?
There is no one but God,
the author
of this life
story
to ask.
And the individuals are that God.
And here I am, also, one of those individuals. One of God's
branches, you might say, if you spoke.
Or sing, like the earliest
musical instruments
all made from trees
the tree
a witness
to all this telling,
Or bloom, in the quiet
sensuality of night whereby other trees
come to know
you. Or are you afraid of what you believe

is witchery? When God
sends lightning down to strike, the fire will burn the tree
first. This, you know
to be true
because it is logical
like a ledger.
But why not ask
questions?
About the violence of math
how it collects
culls.
Ask
what kind of humans
document
the length
of time
another human
survives being burnt alive. Ask
if this is the kind of human
you want to be. The answering
is God's
work or witches'. Gods
and witches have this in common.

The women are burned in a building near the tree . . .
The women are burned beneath the tree . . .
The women are burned hanging from the tree . . .

The tree and I have something in common.
The tree has its own narrative
of death. It knows the bodies burning. I don't know if this story
is true
but it has been repeated
so often that it is. In that way, it was made it true.
This is the work

of old wives. Witches.
The tree and I have something in common.
The tree
is hollow at its base. In this story
that means it has a womb.
Children swing from it. In this story
that means it is a mother. Hollow does not mean empty. What does
    that hollow hold?
Do not be afraid to ask.
Or do be afraid. Either way, there in the tree are the documents
you seek. They are written
in the ancient
languages
of sea water, river water, well water, rain.

The tree and I have something in common.
I am the documents
you seek.

Rowan Ricardo Phillips

Postlude

      Her hospital bed, her favorite red gown,

     the one embroidered with small purple

     and gold flowers trellising the unknown

       infection riddling every inch of her,

    her hair brushed back but not braided today,

     the lunch tray remaindered to a corner,

      plastic pudding cup, nectarine, jaded

    pillbox, all hollowed out, verbless, she sang,

     didn't sing, and sang as she cross-faded

      to an invisible dimension seen

     only on the back of her closed lids,

     the flowers sitting on the windowsill,

    those photos pinned to the wall, the turquoise

    vase, the unused frames, suddenly they seemed

    important, where would they all go, I surprised

myself that, for just a second, I'd deemed

those things to be of value in themselves,

all that flared bric-a-brac, and felt ashamed:

I held her hand in search of some resolve

but as her hand trembled my hand trembled,

I was bad at this, I wanted to prove

that I wasn't, my mind reassembled

and, for a moment, shut down; I joined her

where Charon sat at a makeshift table

killing time with his dog in the foyer,

playing dominoes by himself, waiting

under the faint spectral light of a coy star;

she was there only in the most craven

sense of the word "there," as when someone says

I'll be there soon when they're still in New Haven,

she squeezed my hand and whistled from the strain,

I rubbed her hand with my free hand, then kissed

it, and then kissed her warm forehead again

as I pried my hand from her grip and missed

my last chance not to have done that, I looked

at the time and saw I had a minute

left, then, took a breath I can never take

back after having done all the math, far

away was a better me who would say

she saw it coming so she left, but my car

was waiting downstairs, silver and fine-free,

so I left, the rental purred as I turned

it on, and just like that she was gone.

Maurice Manning

A Penitentiary Rocking Chair

—for Robert Boswell

I don't know what he was guilty of,
the little man who made the chair
back in the nineteenth century
workshop with vises and blocks
and iron hoops for bending the arms,
a drowsy guard perched on a stool
made by prisoners as well,
and outside the timeless river
rolling along before being
swallowed by the father of waters,
the Indian name for the muddy heart
of the country. The ladder back is long
and receives the back of the sitter's head
serenely. The elemental rocking
continues in the maw of Time,
and the hearth-fire dazzles the room.
I went to the prison as a boy
to see the yellow electric chair—
it had a nickname I forget—
and later there's a photograph
of me perched on the lip of the pit
nearby and behind, as if preserved
in a permanent past, is the steam shovel,
the famous, one-of-a-kind machine,
as tall as the Statue of Liberty
and taller, that soon outlived its life
of growing ever underground
and, lurching over, it buried itself.
The dead machinery of death.
The chair creaks and I watch the fire
to imagine this keyhole dot

of Time. Light from the other side
is peeking through and the room is lit.
The little man back there is still
alive with his sleeves rolled up.
A tiny nail had worked its way
out of the wood but I tacked it back.
Poplar slats and hickory stretchers,
light as a feather and sturdy strong.
The language to describe this thing
made by a man forever unknown.
The vision to imagine him
while rocking in the chair he made,
arms on the arms embracing me,
and a question thought though not uttered,
about freedom and what it means,
and then the image of the river
comes to mind and the silence of it,
and not the irony of history,
but the plain, unyielding irony of Time.

Hay-rake

The seat was big enough for two
and my feet couldn't reach the rests
and the reins were invisible when I jerked
them in the air and lightly clucked
to persuade the imaginary horse
to make his way into the field
and rake the imaginary hay
first into rows and then into ricks.
There was a lever to the right
and a few notches in a wheel
to let the rib-cage of tines
lightly reach the ground and rake
the hay, though only rusted iron
by now, the lever was only a thing
I pretended to move. I pretended
my way all over the field, and then
I pretended to have a barn to fill,
but the old equipment didn't move.
And the field was just a patch of ground
with briars where a fence had been.
Sometimes if the ground was dry
I'd crawl into the tunnel of tines
and look up at the sky, or pretend
it was now the third hot day
and all I was was a field of hay.

The Golden Treachery of Poetry

I've got a yodel and a-half
another yodel inside of me,
and a verse or two of tweedle-dee
to run a possum up a tree,
or just to make a dandy noise
for occasions when I use my voice
as if it were a harmonickee,
and now and then I find repose
by strumming my fingers against my nose
and, humming melodiously, I free
the one-stringed banjo that lives
beside the yodel and a-half
I keep in me and the verse or two
of tweedle-dee, and, of course I save
some room for serious poetry,
because I believe, my friends, in Beauty
with a capital B and Dirt with a D,
but a banjo in a serious poem,
or a poem searching for Truth with a T,
may cause the poem to fall just short
of perfection, or encourage the poet
to resolve the poem by claiming he
can do a convincing imitation
of a chicken practicing the art
of silence in moody contemplation.

Heather Hamilton

But out Loud

Dead flies lay jacketed
in jeweled iridescence
between the window glass
and the peeling sill,
newly visible now that
the blinds were gone,
and all around them
wallpaper pears,
suspended in perfect ripeness,
blushed burgundy.
It was the summer
of helping friends
move, and then
never hearing from them
again, except
through other friends
who hadn't shown,
the summer I began
to wonder if friendship
is only about pleasure,
not service, and if
I would ever
understand it fully,
even when lifting
banker's boxes
of someone else's books.
To be only partially fluent
In neurotypical is
to be shut out,
but almost not,
like the flies who thought,
until the very end,
that they could cross

over through the glass.
So many invisible
wires buzzing overhead.
So many things
that would take flight
if done with more iridescence.
We should get together soon,
we all said, which is
a way of saying nothing,
but out loud.

Sylvia Jones

Generational Conflict

My grandmas' kids threw out

her cookbooks that were living

in a shed behind the house

next to the wooden palette on cinder blocks

where we used to stack firewood

wearing oven mitts.

A chain-gang of nieces and nephews

who eventually will stretch into an amalgam

of troublesome, successful, and worrisome

adults, all of whom don't even cook.

Can't cook. Couldn't cook

to save their lives.

Bob Kaufman Like Tendencies

My mom doesn't know

who Bob Kaufman is

so she'll think

this is an homage

to her dead ex-husband, my former,

now late stepfather

who once attempted

to get me and my brother

(when we were minors)

to invest

in a Ponzi scheme

with our confirmation

money

Ned Balbo

Redemptions in Stained Glass

—On discovering my birth father's projects online.

Father who raised my brothers, father known
    as scarcely kin, father who summoned
fortune from hardship but forfeited the son
    and daughter who, like contraband,
    would bear a false name and pretend—

Father we viewed, resigned, from separate houses,
    father whose glassworks shook with noise
and smelled of solder, father of troubled causes
    cruel to hired men; whose voice
    resolved or silenced any choice—

Father who now works calmly in stained glass,
    pendant of waterfowl in flight
adorning a picture window; father who'll pass
    long hours grinding shapes that light
    will touch to color and ignite—

Father whose lamplit dragonflies, lead-edged,
    are glazed in gold; whose sunlit door
weaves peacock feathers, petals his vision salvaged
    into iridescence; father
    who's finally had his fill of power,

perhaps, tracing new patterns on a light box;
    handling glass with gloved hands, clearing
shards away with care, peering past flecks
    of paint and flux on goggles, fearing
    nothing, whole days disappearing

into the moment, far from memory—
    Father whose past, not spoken of,
may surface still when memory starts to stray,
    whose pain was always keen enough—
    The same father my brothers love.

> —Note: The stanza derives from George Herbert's "The Windows." My sister and I are a year apart in age; to conceal the scandal that our birth parents were not yet married to each other, we were raised in separate households under assumed names. (Our younger brothers were born after the marriage had taken place.)

Nazifa Islam

How to Write Poems

> —*a found poem: The Unabridged Journals of Sylvia Plath*

Start the poem with conflict.
The bird can't fly.

It won't. Or start it with a revelation.
God is like other men—

full of excuses. Begin tangling
thoughts. *Life fragments*

the mind. Fear & jealousy
are not useless.

Make the decision to become
emotional. *The baby*

can't move.
Lorelai is hanging herself tomorrow.

Put aside what I consider
alien subjects:

romance, courtship, marriage.
Always invoke

a phobia of time. Extend the page.
Think. Think. Writing

is a green wash of exhaustion.
Start to know this.

Bohemian

    —a found poem: The Unabridged Journals of Sylvia Plath

The world's breaking in two
and I am
continually reshaping myself

with my writing.
I crack open, I shake, I feel
more & more intolerable

panic; I remember everything.
But I also amass figments
of unheard sound

concentrate on the few things
that are invaluable—
writing, reading, making—

have a clear sense of myself.
I am not paralyzed
by this nightmare of a life.

I must write
to bear my own steady growth.
I know I can do this. I have to.

Poetry is a detonation—a welter
of art, cold fears
and all that is possible.

Whole and Human

—a found poem: The Unabridged Journals of Sylvia Plath

Find your way back to the vital hour when your mother—growing old
in a rusty blue shack by the harbor with light trickling in
streams down the windows—cried
because of the beauty of the new flowers sitting in the yellow grass.
This was a kind of wild love beyond that of blood and kin
and you can carry it in you forever.

Hílda Davis

J'ouvert, 2012

& so it is,
when you & your friends want to get on bad,
you get on bad, & if you do not know what getting
on bad means, then this here event is not
for you—the hands, slathered
in paint, slapping bare breasts, & nearly
bare asses in the rain, & we do not know
what song the band is playing right now, but
we know we have been trained for years to share a handle
of rum with just one friend, because that is how
one loosens the waist, think of rum as the rhythm's oil, yes,
we all know the body must be able to
rotate like hands on a clock, hour after hour
over one another, & here, we have no idea
what time it is, three A.M. is like three P.M. when everyone
is so radiant, the liquor, warmth causing us all to flash our
teeth so hard, everyone is convinced they are
happy, or in love, & once after pelting my waist against his through,
who knows how many songs, because what are songs & what is
time when you have the first weekend in September & Eastern Parkway
& so much Black & delicious mess all to yourself—
a man says he wants to marry me, asks me my name & where
I am from, I say *Ebony, Jamaica,* & neither is my
name or land of origin—when the half
handle of rum finally catches up to you, sometimes
all you can remember is your color;
where your gran is laid to rest

Amorak Huey

Autumn

If a season had a mouth—
if it had fingers—
or if its warmth were teeth.

Darling

Almost immediately,
in our first moments
on this planet, we learn
to turn our faces
toward what we desire.
We spend our lives
repeating this gesture.
This morning, a late snow,
and I lift my eyes
to the icy sky.
Save this under beauty.
Save it under hope.

Nigh

Four days until the end of the world
I wish I were exaggerating
Four days to loot what treasure we can from each other
Fingers in skin
Four days to dig
First pleasure
Then grave

Don Bogen

From the Valley Floor

> —*Martinez, February*

1.
Morning drizzle through a window:
raindrops, against the gray-white sky, invisible.
Against the trees ghostly, a veil or fog.

*

Steady rain pulls me inward—
the past rises as the hills blur out in gray.
So much behind me, and my path just a ramble near the creek bed.
I won't be long.

*

I can't recall anything I saw on my walk—
it's all so familiar it becomes transparent:
the long straight road a chute to loss and brooding,
the past a pit, the future hanging over it
a low cloud of tasks left unfinished.

*

Only when I get this done, I thought, and that, and that.
Only when the kids are, the house is, only when,
only when the ramble's over.

* * * * *

2.
They took out the line of eucalyptus along the creek bank
because, in a fire, the trees could explode.
Ridiculous exotics: their wood too weak to be useful,
their oil inflammable—but fragrant,
its scent a gate to lost summers.

*

I am lying on a bench in that grove on campus fifty years ago,
looking up at the spindly leaves and strips of bark spinning,
my smile fixed, heart packed with joy.

*

After a night of showers, the light looks wrung.
The air, rich with ozone, makes me think I can run forever.
Wisps, puffballs, shifting arrays of gray and white—
these clouds remind me of Ireland.

*

The past keeps churning up shards.
Wisconsin is numinous interiors glazed with nostalgia:
a dance studio in someone's basement,
the dim light and too-heavy mahogany chairs of the library
on a late afternoon with snow in the air.

*

I am in that place and this:
a child looking out from a small-town library
and a man staring through a window at a dripping tree.

* * * * *

3.
The creek tells the valley what the highest hills heard.
The fuller it grows, the louder it sounds.
As it gathers, it dips underground
then opens in a channel beneath bridges, slows, and spreads into
      wetlands:
a thousand voices murmuring at once.

*

Hills low here, where the valley broadens to marsh.
Cattails and pepperweed in damp air.
Few trees: the odd stumpy palm,
a grove of eucalyptus some settler planned to harvest for timber.

*

Dawn glinting off water, sharpened shadow,
each in its own way obliterating detail
as the bay itself swallows the muttering creek.

*

Light, sudden, on wet bark—
raw light, the cloud cover torn off,
the sycamore in the backyard pocked and soaking.
Brown and gray beneath every color of the bark:
color of sand, color of clay, color of dirt.

*

The sun says *Look here, and here* for just a second
then calms to warm the whole tree uniformly,
the wet bark steaming.

* * * * *

4.
I could see just the tip of a plane tree poking up
behind the wall I'd stare at in Belfast
as I watched the soft rain come and go, come and go,
drops on the crumbling brick swelling to fall,
and made a song of it.

*

Yellow-green moss on the pear limb fierce and gleaming,
a carpet of small, hooked tendrils,
this stick all it needs for soil.

*

In a scroll I saw on a museum wall
poets are writing messages to float on rice-paper boats.
The creek takes up whole panels drifting them downstream
where others stoop, pluck out the messages,
and read, clapping for joy.

*

Bureaucrats at play a dozen centuries ago.
The scene lively, evocative, fixed in ink,
horizontal to give an illusion of time.

*

If the future holds no set course in the time stream,
it never arrives.
If the past exists only as a concept,
memory's a trick of mind.

*

Entropy turned all those moments—
turned those *in* them—
more detailed at first,
then smaller, more broken and numerous:
flakes of ash, dispersed.

     * * * * *

5.
On a morning run, looking ahead:
When I get back the rain will start to come down steadily,
and I'll stare out the window thinking it will never stop.

     *

The pear transmutes this steady breeze to a thousand motions.
Water beads hang on the branch tips till they fall.
Twigs, buds dotting the new limbs
among the clumps of stiff black leaves—
everything going up and down and back and forth at once.

     *

When the furnace isn't running,
I hear raindrops drumming on the roof,
the pattern so intricate it blurs into a hush.
What could they be saying but *Listen, Listen?*

Jane Lewty

Clairvoyant City Triptych

i.

Look, the troposphere has stopped all the waves. There is movement
 around us.
A tranquil light that isn't so. Strewn summer wind
a slant building—photo felt on arrival, old stone.
Everywhere is as-I-thought, will I ever get used to? I could promenade
short-cut, stream into wherever, say: *hello, I'm OTW.*
Messages only work if you live in isolation, and are you?
Apparently, we must resist the embrace of those who have lost.
 Resist the guide of wasted time:
its track from window-to-window, gently, ineluctably.
Soon, we'll sit in quiet bargaining by a kind-of water
the words being, *what if We were home?*
Then, I'll almost run a figure eight, keeping or consuming, what
I'm not sure. Either way, by way of co-conscious I was in several places:
I was lying down; I was standing up; I was keenly pushing ahead
with codas mapped out. Codas to everything.
Look at us now / then / here, our landscape set.
Our tone so rootless and very glad for it.
Afterwards silent in a kitchen, a kitchen I will come to know.
And the singleness of every minute in its walls that seemed like, what?
 Like my dream.
I waited in your night. I was bloodless. I was there.

ii.

As if someone slid open a screen
silently closing it before the view
can be understood—
here, in this car, here is noise*like*
Vision*like*. We glide through

the buzzing fields of a city, the east of it, in
quiet of dis-structured day
Its angles watching &
watchful as the strange audio clarity of lifeless water:
compound slow-ers of no-sound, crescendo then decay.
You look
says the driver, *like a man whose oil tankers are on fire*
A figure-to-be
with falling sorrow whose riches are gone. Futureless face staring
while a visible bleed
kills near-surface creatures: benzene
toluthene, xylene . . . . *I know*—the reply—*Due to dream and want
there is something, and I cannot get beyond it.*
At 2pm the city is unlighted, unthought-of, it lies
in parts afar & how we know its arteries through rear-side
view-side, mirror-side. All this outering. Glissandi
from 'A' to 'B'
Then back to 'A' in the scrapping dark
keenly joyous & fleeting-syllable-malleable. *But you look*, says the driver
Your expression looks like—
Can you put your passages in a mouth? Do you know how
distant your harmony is, how
you skim over the contours of life—its colors *like*
oil fractions settling on the slow-tide
a slick foil to the sun?
And those vessels—their bolt & plunge & burden: *my investment
my fleet*, my hyper-adrift form, my love. We smile at
these imaginary horizons. He says one last time: *you look
like someone who has lost it all.*
We are here—the street is a bank of water.
The car slows. The ocean burns.
Try again: Perhaps there is a fire, and I cannot get beyond it.

iii.

We're eavesdropping—under a roof with vapor outside
a hose coiled and rivulet. Waves of speech or intent leasing out
spread then confined
in a way that holds us. One of us will be poised, an angel on a high wire.
One of us watches a creature tear at the ground, saying *Look up*
look up from wherever your foot happens to fall. One of us will track light
        back & forth
across the garden. Some of us are sad.
Sad & confined, so sad.
Cleansed in some form and not in others.
As for me, I bear all weight, bear all desire.
We'll hear the woman's voice: high-rising, raw, similar: *"I am sorry for that"*
Like me, she is sorry that this series of extended or stretched words
has given rise to
the question of ambiguity of heart-sounds.

Felicia Zamora

To Put Meat Back

You stand in pajamas, *haaaw* out your breath
to the sharp morning & count the scarlet
robins in perch of branches—drops of blood
on finger bones—an end, like a synapse
slides into the crevasses of your cells; aren't we
always transmitting in response to impulse
here among the gray atmosphere, trees crack
wood lightening into the gravestone clouds
hide the myth of permanent cessation, secret
to regeneration, what we forget when doused
in infections & over a million lost & moratoriums
& unemployment rivals 1929-1939 & a nation
hesitates to crack its knuckles, to put meat back
on this skeleton before the winter licks us dry.

Monopoly

The ship. I always wanted the ship. Tight to play the ship. & that Ol' shoe. Stank. & trust me, Fry's words—*What smells like boot feet?*—from *Futurama* scroll through my head, butter on hot corn. & yes Matt Groening cartoons mythically find ways into my poems. Don't they yours? I quote *The Simpsons* intimately like a twelve-year-old 90's boy with his twelve-year-old friends. Roll the accusations in hurl at my feminism, or loose feminism, or "bad" to pay homage to Gay's insurmountable genius. Let me love on women in this poem; juxtapose embraces of estrogen right next to Homer, not the epic one, well, not that kind of epic, that plump & sunflower icon of my childhood living inside me still. Gay, I couldn't agree more on how nostalgia fixates inside the gelatinous curves & creases of the brain.

In the news, the Justice Department files a lawsuit against Google. The US government, this country, our governing body with broken judicial systems, hiring god-complexed politicians to sever basic human rights from marginalized populations, claims an unlawful monopoly on Google over— power. Power over internet searches and, surprise surprise, internet advertising. Oh, Capitalism, you barbed-wire heart of this nation, scraping at cells & flesh & bleeding us from the inside out. Capitalism, you leak in the hull unable to patch yourself, unable to scoop the rising water out of your guts so you toss the life preservers over, pock holes in life rafts to ensure you don't go down alone. Capitalism, you tantrum throwing child with the remote yelling, *Fuck Rose & her comfortable British UN seat. Fuck Jack, for being in poverty* (& how you ignore your hand in socio-economic class & how you only watch movies with white actors . . . like we don't notice.) Are antitrust actions against Google unnecessary, Lemieux? Is internet dominance temporary? Who's keeping whom safe? Golden age of Noir & again we piecemeal in black & white. Temporary dominance alludes to the players ability to mutate the game. Game board pieces circling & revolting. Game of a game—never being asked, a forcing. Thimble, dog, wheelbarrow, top hat, iron: objects. The way a country sees humanity. Who am I kidding? I always knew the ship meant a battleship.

Jessa Queyrouze

Teeth

Your dentist can tell you were poor as a child.
Your water from a well, your teeth the chalky white
of powdered milk. (In your dreams they come unmoored,
they drop like dice. The guilt of it lingers, sick
in your gut, long after you wake.) The careful scrape, the tiny
fishhook at your tender gum line. This one has to come out, he says.

Your parents used to be cool. Hallowed.
Long-haired, the slick, bright sheen of records in a crate,
Oyster shell ashtray, mother of pearl, thick with nicotine—
a photograph gone hazy gold with age. (That old trick.)
Your father's slim-boned, freckled feet. Those genes,
repeating. Your parents probably used to be cool.

Your own children now, asleep down the hall, breathing
lightly as ghosts. (Breathe.) Their own teeth
glinting. Years ago, before their births, those hard-won
tattered minerals, leached and stolen by the sluice
of your own salty blood, and re-emerging, pearl by pearl
in the tight bud of each baby's waiting mouth.

Hollowed out. You cracked your ravaged coccyx once,
eight months pregnant, slamming a door. Bleached and branched,
the white coral you dropped and broke, as a careless child,
on your mother's bathroom tile. You sobbed too hard to catch your breath.
Everything is fragile. Bird boned, eggshell crunch, each baby birthed
came squalling. Each clamshell nursing grip. Pinched.

The tooth cracks when he pulls it.
(Swirl of anesthesia, salty ether, smoke and mirrors.
That old trick.) You hear it click into the bowl, a pair of dice,
two clicks. He says—you're brushing too much,
you're too rough. Enough. The gentlest shaming. Face flush,
the room, the record spins. Deep breath. Enough, enough.

Louise Ling Edwards

Grandmother's Eggroll Recipe

1. Use wonton skins instead of eggroll skins. There is less to work with. You never knew your grandmother, didn't know how to fit into her name. You are a mess of languages.

2. Get the French-cut green beans. It will make the severing process easier. The process of cutting you from you. Mince up everything small so that it will fit inside the skin: garlic, green onion, ginger, ground beef or substitute mushrooms to avoid butchering.

3. Get the proportions right. You will want to jam everything in to maximize flavor, but your skin might explode. Take a smaller spoonful.

4. Dip your fingers into warm water and run them along the edges of dough. Bind with hot tears—yours or your grandmother's. The homesickness, the craving for something, anything Chinese.

5. Fold and fold and fold in. Seal up contents like an envelope licked by the tongue of an ancestor. Make sure there are no holes. The insides might escape.

6. Corn oil is best. Your dad has taught you. The oil is ready when it speaks: sputters and pops. You are oil and water. You are sting and kiss. You are droplets thrown to a place you didn't know you could exist. The river of the faucet heals a scalding ache.

7. Fry. Miss the way your grandmother fished the eggrolls out with chopsticks. Graceful stork legs wading in lava. Hands brave and trembling. You have never even seen your grandmother's hands.

8. You cannot make eggrolls alone. Folding, wrapping, holding: you have to share the labor. You have to love the same way my grandmother loved me. Without knowing there was anything to love. Just knowing everyone must be fed and full.

Subhaga Crystal Bacon

Parsing the Nonbinary

I'm wearing a man's shirt,
man's watch and boots and belt.
My hair hangs to my waist,
my eyelids lined in a color called *rough*.

                              Rough trade the bodies I yearned for.
                   Tongue down throat, knee between thighs.
                        Is this color the come hither look
                              I use to pick out my eyes?

I've never been so confused
about who I am. My friends
used to say I was a gay man
trapped in a lesbian's body.

                     Gay   *man*   *lesbian*
                                  What language is that?
                             Words pointing to an idea
                        that's nothing to do with body.

Is my body a rough
approximation of beauty?
I only know it where language
is silenced, naming, defunct.

        *

I thought I was a boy until puberty,
was warned that I would turn
into a boy if I didn't *change*,
stop wanting a bulge in my pants.

                    I was not afraid. I remember a silk blouse
                printed with elephants and mice, permed hair;
                            then and later, a kind of drag
                                as in *disguise* and *trial*.

      *

A child I knew seven years ago,
who was then someone's daughter,
under a new name, *Alex, they/them*
still beams the same light.

                    In our middle school, six nonbinary kids,
                            born *female*. I feel the safety
                        of being nonbinary at puberty. Saying:
                                keep your ideas off my body.

In my family, we have a child, *she/her,*
who at seven only answered to *Finn.*
Cut her hair; wore her brother's clothes:
the joy of being taken for a boy.

      *

I used to say *woman can look like this.*
And it's still true. Man, woman, female,
male, only sounds to limit what is true in us.
They, them, theirs living free in the both/and.

                            It's Shakespearian; I'm a man
                        disguised as a woman playing a boy.
                        What a precious, private thing it is.
                            She/they/them. I am who I am.

Gregory Djanikian

What Is It We Said

I can't remember, but it was something
that deserved significant thought
which I think we gave it
as night slowly descended

though that was yesterday
and now there's a black hole
where a constellation of words
used to wheel and spin

but I remember you said them
with a certain irrepressible spirit
your hands gesturing wildly
as if they were uncaged birds

and the willow outside
shaking forcefully by the window
in a sudden swirl of wind
we were immune to

because we kept on talking
until everything made so much sense
that you said write it down
and I said I'll remember

which of course I didn't
and how desperately I think back now
to that night's *tabula rasa*
we were fervently marking up

as we listened to the cicadas outside
soughing in a loud chorus of dissonant song

thinking it a miracle that they remember
what to declare night after night

filling up the world
with so much noise and congregation,
what we wanted to do and did
even though we've lost the sense of it now

every sumptuous phrase
every word spoken as if
it was one of many breaths
we were giving to each other.

Instructions for a Disappearance

If you feel you'd like to say
goodbye to the world,
do it slowly, giving birdsongs
a chance to twine in your ear,
the dogs to nuzzle up to your palm
with their wet noses.

If you're in the woods
and wish to lie down at last
under pine needles and leaves,
try to feel the moistness of the soil,
how so many roots are intertwined
below your arms and calves.

Let the ocean take you if you wish,
the white foam curling into the blue,
but remember the billions of years it has taken you
to walk deeply into the water
as if you were invited back.

If you wish to see how heavy you are
against the upthrust of air,
you must stand on the crest of a mountain
feeling the low clouds
misting your body
the ethereal brushing against
the sublime congealment of skin.

Take a breath and maybe
you'll breathe in some small part of the world
that might make you feel at home.

If not, then there's nothing left to do
but to construe your disappearance
as a mystery, the sudden stoppage
of life coming abruptly, but the dispersal
of body and mind and spirit

continuing bit by bit, atom by atom,
percolating into the ground,
leaching into the air and water,
until, in time, you will be part
of what, for you, has seemed unendurable,
and nothing will be left of you
but the breadth of the entire earth itself.

Zebulon Huset

Universally Remote

Lost in the Narnia between couch cushions
or eaten by the dog let in last thunderstorm.
Placed somewhere distant in space and we
rode earth's orbit away from it once more.
Once, we were a slave to the original maker
of our televisions. With lost remote control,
it was off-the-couch-on-the-couch-off-again
to avoid annoyingly pandering advertising
with only slightly less annoyingly pandering
program content. It satisfied our software
where the hard truth of wallet and its lack
made the super slip-n-slide castle so painful
to see. The select few played feudal house
and we were dragged into their games of
high stakes Monopoly without any of our own
Life boards to shield ourselves from punishment.
From their inflatable ivory castle we looked
ignorant and dirty, poor. Kept at bay by mote.
So we re-moted, protecting our distant mudhill.
Mud, all our own! Then the microwave struck
TV Dinner o'clock and the glories of the new
remote that worked with almost any television.
The miracles of science like those which brought
crushed ice in refrigerator doors and Walkmen
to make isolation so much more convenient. Sure,
the inflatable castle caste had VCRs with timers
that didn't always say midnight and they stuck
with their programs, merely fast forwarding
over less desirable bits of tv doctrine. But, too,
with their oversized universal remote which also
controlled their laser disc player. They're split too.
Our molecules like pixels building this moment
in some rear-projection existence, baying selfhood

into the dark and letting SETI listen in case a beam
from some remote corner of the universe wants
to share *their* entertainment with us, for once.

The Cutting Room Floor

Whirlpools of time steal from me
like the conmen culling calendars
of any meaning but ticked boxes.
I remember the lilacs of Mays past,
the solitude of lunchtime munching
a mom-made sandwich in the hall
betterment band practice rooms
where no one interrupted my roost,
the nights when dad let me watch
Carson or Monty Python, the dark
early mornings in thin aluminum
fishing boat so small we could heft
it, empty, into his old pick up bed.
I remember many shifts as victual
courier, many turns as amateur
croupier for the neighborhood boys
roughly my age—plastic poker chips
our imaginary currency along with
mass-produced baseball cards: Topps,
Fleer, Upper Deck, Stadium Club . . .
But the memories are smooth stones
skipping on the pond surface near
Grandma's farm up north, snippets
of far larger days, longer documentaries
cut down from hundreds of thousands
of hours of raw footage, unknown
pounds of lost film left on the cutting
room floor without even knowing

they'd been snipped from the reel.
This is the way of things. Sunsets
and sad playlists, poignant moments
along with dull ones slip far away.
The rear view mirror selectively fogged
by the evening's humidity, by the vast
distances in both time and space.

Poetry Prizes

22nd Annual Erskine J. Poetry Prize

First Prize: Miasma—**Christopher Childers** (page 1)

Second Prize: Conspiracy Song—**Austin Allen** (page 66)

Third Prize: From the Valley Floor—**Don Bogen** (page 99)

Finalists
    Redemptions in Stained Glass—**Ned Balbo** (page 92)
    To a Foster Mother—**Matt Hohner** (page 36)
    Universally Remote & The Cutting Room Floor
        —**Zebulon Huset** (page 117)
    Apostle—**David Moolten** (page 38)

Prize Judge: **Stephen Reichert**

19th Annual Beullah Rose Poetry Prize

First Prize: Strange Math, Dickinson—**Eva Heisler** (page 30)

Second Prize: After Seshadri's "Cliffhanging"
    —**Elizabeth Hazen** (page 34)

Third Prize: Parsing the Nonbinary
    —**Subhaga Crystal Bacon** (page 112)

Finalists
    Grandmother's Eggroll Recipe—**Louise Ling Edwards** (page 111)
    On a Sticky Cow-Lying Summer Afternoon in 1947
        —**Eva Heisler** (page 32)
    J'ouvert, 2012—**Hílda Davis** (page 97)
    Teeth—**Jessa Queyrouze** (page 110)

Prize Judge: **Traci O'Dea**

Contributors

KIM ADDONIZIO has published over a dozen books of poetry and prose. Her latest poetry collection is Now We're Getting Somewhere (2021) and forthcoming is Exit Opera, both from W.W. Norton. Tell Me (BOA, 2000) was National Book Award finalist. She offers poetry workshops on Zoom and teaches and performs at various conferences and festivals.

AUSTIN ALLEN's debut poetry collection, *Pleasures of the Game* (Waywiser, 2016), was awarded the Anthony Hecht Poetry Prize. He has studied and taught creative writing at Johns Hopkins University and the University of Cincinnati.

LAURA AMUSSEN is a faculty member at Towson University and the Maryland Institute College of Art. Her work has been widely exhibited, most recently as a Baker Artist Awardee she created a large-scale, site-specific installation titled *Forest Royalty* for the Baltimore Museum of Art (2023) and as sculptor-in-residence at Ladew Topiary Gardens (2020).

RAE ARMANTROUT is the author of seventeen books of poetry including *Versed* (Wesleyan, 2009), winner of the Pulitzer Prize and The National Book Critics Circle Award; *Wobble* (Wesleyan, 2018), a finalist for the National Book Award; and *Finalists* (Wesleyan, 2022). Retired from UC San Diego where she was professor of poetry and poetics, she is the current judge of the Yale Younger Poets Prize.

SUBHAGA CRYSTAL BACON is the author of four collections of poetry including *Surrender of Water in Hidden Places* (2023), winner of the Red Flag Poetry Chapbook Prize, and *Transitory*, recipient of the Isabella Gardner Award for Poetry, forthcoming in the fall of 2023 from BOA Editions.

NED BALBO is the author of six poetry collections including *The Cylburn Touch-Me-Nots* (New Criterion, 2019) and *3 Nights of the Perseids* (U. of Evansville, 2019), winner of the Richard Wilbur Award, whose title poem appears in the Cambridge University Press anthology *Outer Space: 100 Poems* (2022). His book, *The Trials of Edgar Poe and Other Poems* (Story Line, 2010), received the Donald Justice Prize and the 2012 Poets' Prize. He has received grants or fellowships from the National Endowment for the Arts (translation) and the Maryland State Arts Council.

DON BOGEN is the author of five books of poetry, most recently *Immediate Song* (Milkweed, 2019). An emeritus professor at the University of Cincinnati, he serves as editor-at-large for *The Cincinnati Review* and splits his time between Cincinnati and Martinez, CA. His website is donbogen.com.

DANIEL BORZUTZKY is the author of six books of poetry, most recently *Written After a Massacre in the Year 2018* (Coffee House, 2021). *The Performance of Becoming Human* (Brooklyn Arts, 2016) received the National Book Award and *Lake Michigan* (U. of

Pittsburgh, 2018) was a finalist for the Griffin International Poetry Prize. His translation of Paula Ilabaca Nuñez's *The Loose Pearl* (co-im-press, 2022) won the PEN Award for Poetry in Translation and his translation of Galo Ghigliotto's *Valdivia* (co-im-press, 2016) received ALTA's 2017 National Translation Award. He has also translated collections by Raúl Zurita and Jaime Luis Huenún. A new poetry book, *The Murmuring Grief of the Americas*, is forthcoming from Coffee House Press.

CHRISTOPHER CHILDERS has published poems, essays and translations in *Agni, Literary Matters, The Dark Horse, The Kenyon Review, The PN Review* and *The Yale Review*. He is the editor of *The Penguin Book of Greek and Latin Lyric Verse* forthcoming from Penguin Classics in November 2023.

HÍLDA DAVIS earned a Master of Fine Arts in creative writing from New York University, and her work has been featured in *Callaloo* and *The Offing*. A poet and essayist from Staten Island, NY, Davis currently resides in Seattle, WA.

GREGORY DJANIKIAN has published seven poetry collections with Carnegie Mellon University Press, the latest of which is *Sojourners of the In-Between* (2020), which includes a poem that first appeared in *Smartish Pace*. He is at work on a New and Selected compilation.

LOUISE LING EDWARDS is a poet and essayist who has lived in St. Paul, MN and rural China in Shanxi Province. Currently, she resides in Columbus, OH where she received her MFA from The Ohio State University. The 2022 winner of the Walter Rumsey Marvin Grant from the Ohioana Library Association, Edward's work is forthcoming in *Ninth Letter*.

PETER GRANDBOIS is the author of fourteen books, most recently *Domestic Bestiary* (Spuyten Duyvil, 2022). His plays have been performed in St. Louis, Columbus, Los Angeles and New York. He is poetry editor of *Boulevard* and teaches at Denison University in Ohio.

RACHEL HADAS is the author of twenty-three books of poetry and essays; her most recent poetry collections are *Love and Dread* (Measure, 2021) and *Pandemic Almanac* (Ragged Sky, 2022). *Ghost Guest* is forthcoming later this year from Ragged Sky Press. Her honors include a Guggenheim Fellowship, Ingram Merrill Foundation Grants, the O.B. Hardison Award from the Folger Shakespeare Library and an Award in Literature from the American Academy and Institute of Arts and Letters.

HEATHER HAMILTON's chapbook, *Here is a Clearing*, was published in 2019 by the Poetry Society of America. She is a graduate of the creative writing PhD program at the University of Cincinnati, where she received an Academy of American Poets prize, and now teaches at Penn State Harrisburg.

JARED HARÉL is the author of *Go Because I Love You* (Diode, 2018) and *Let Our Bodies Change the Subject* (U. of Nebraska, 2023), winner of the 2022 Raz/Shumaker Prairie Schooner Book Prize in Poetry. Winner of the Stanley Kunitz Memorial Prize from *American Poetry Review* and the William Matthews Poetry Prize from *Asheville Poetry Review*, Harél teaches at The Writers Circle, plays drums for the NYC-based rock band *Flyin' J & The Ghostrobber* and lives with his family in Westchester, NY.

ELIZABETH HAZEN has published two collections of poetry: *Chaos Theories* (2016) and *Girls Like Us* (2020). Her work was a finalist for the 2005 Beullah Rose Prize from *Smartish Pace* and appeared in *Best American Poetry 2013* (Scribner).

EVA HEISLER has published two books of poetry: *Reading Emily Dickinson in Icelandic* (Kore, 2013) and *Drawing Water* (Noctuary, 2013). Her honors include the Poetry Society of America's Emily Dickinson Award and fellowships at MacDowell and Millay Arts. She was co-winner of the 2021 Poetry International Prize.

MATT HOHNER's poetry has won multiple international poetry competitions. He is the recipient of two residencies at the Virginia Center for the Creative Arts and a forthcoming residency at Anam Cara Retreat in Ireland. An editor of *Loch Raven Review*, Hohner wrote a first collection of poems titled *Thresholds and Other Poems* (Apprentice House, 2018).

AMORAK HUEY is the author of four books of poems including *Dad Jokes from Late in the Patriarchy* (Sundress, 2021). Co-founder of River River Books, Huey teaches writing at Bowling Green State University. He also is co-author of the textbook *Poetry: A Writer's Guide and Anthology* (Bloomsbury, 2018) and *Slash/Slash* (2021), winner of the Diode Editions Chapbook Prize.

ZEBULON HUSET is a teacher, writer and photographer. He won the *Gulf Stream* 2020 Summer Poetry Contest and his writing has appeared in *Best New Poets* (2021, Samovar/Meridian), *Fence*, *North American Review* and *Rattle*. He publishes *Notebooking Daily* and edits the literary journal *Coastal Shelf*.

NAZIFA ISLAM is the author of the poetry collections *Searching for a Pulse* (Whitepoint, 2013) and *Forlorn Light: Virginia Woolf Found Poems* (Shearsman, 2021). She earned her MFA at Oregon State University.

SYLVIA JONES recently served as a 2021-22 Stadler Fellow and is currently an associate editor at Black Lawrence Press while teaching creative writing and composition at Goucher College and The George Washington University. She is a reader for *Ploughshares*, and her most recent work appears in *DIAGRAM*, *Santa Clara Review*, *Shenandoah* and *The Hopkins Review*. She earned her MFA from American University and lives in Baltimore.

JARED JOSEPH lives and writes in Los Angeles. His book, *A Book About Myself Called Hell*, was published by Kernpunkt Press in 2022. His novel, *Danny the Ambulance*, is forthcoming from Outpost19.

CHRISTOPHER KONDRICH is the author of *Contrapuntal* (FreeVerse, 2013) and *Valuing* (U. of Georgia, 2019), a winner of the National Poetry Series. He is Visiting Assistant Professor at the College of the Holy Cross and teaches in Eastern Oregon University's low-residency MFA program.

EDGAR KUNZ is the author of two collections of poetry: *Tap Out* (Mariner, 2019) and *Fixer* (Ecco, 2023). He has been a National Endowment for the Arts Fellow, a MacDowell Fellow and a Wallace Stegner Fellow at Stanford University. He lives in Baltimore and teaches at Goucher College.

DAVID LEHMAN is the author of sixteen poetry books, including *Playlist* (U. of Pittsburgh, 2019), and nine nonfiction books, including *One Hundred Autobiographies: A Memoir* (Cornell U., 2019). Series editor for *The Best American Poetry*, Lehman as a journalist had writings in *Art in America, Newsweek, People, Smithsonian, The New York Times* and *The Wall Street Journal*. From 1997 to 2003, he co-hosted the KGB Bar poetry series and co-edited *The KGB Bar Book of Poems* (HarperCollins, 2000).

LYNN LEVIN's fifth poetry collection, *The Minor Virtues* (Ragged Sky, 2020), was listed as one of 2020's best books by *The Philadelphia Inquirer*. Her debut collection of short fiction is *House Parties* (Spuyten Duyvil, 2023). She teaches at Drexel University.

JANE LEWTY is the author of two collections of poetry: *Bravura Cool* (1913 Press, 2013) and *In One Form To Find Another* (Cleveland State U., 2017). She has co-edited two volumes of essays: *Pornotopias: Image, Desire, Apocalypse* (Litteraria Pragensia, 2009) and *Broadcasting Modernism* (U. of Florida, 2010). She teaches at Maryland Institute College of Art (MICA) and lives in Baltimore.

EMILY LEE LUAN is the author of *I Watch the Boughs* (2021), selected by Gabrielle Calvocoressi for a Poetry Society of America chapbook fellowship, and 回/*Return* (2023), winner of the Nightboat Poetry Prize. A former Margins Fellow at the Asian American Writers' Workshop and the recipient of a Pushcart Prize, Luan wrote poems that appeared in *Best New Poets 2019* (Samovar/Meridian) and *Best American Poetry 2021* (Scribner). She holds an MFA from Rutgers University-Newark.

OKSANA MAKSYMCHUK is the author of poetry collections *Xenia* (Piramida, 2005) and *Lovy* (Smoloskyp, 2008) and a recipient of Bohdan-Ihor Antonych and Smoloskyp prizess. She co-edited *Words for War: New Poems from Ukraine* (Academic Studies/Harvard Ukrainian Research Institute, 2017). She won the Richmond Lattimore and Joseph Brodsky-Stephen Spender translation competitions and an NEA

Translation Fellowship. Maksymchuk is the co-translator of *Apricots of Donbas* (Lost Horse, 2021) by Lyuba Yakimchuk and *The Voices of Babyn Yar* (Harvard U., 2022) by Marianna Kiyanovska. Based in Lviv, Ukraine, she currently resides in Poland.

MAURICE MANNING's eighth book of poetry, *Snakedoctor*, will be published by Copper Canyon this fall. *The Common Man* (Houghton Mifflin Harcourt, 2010) was a 2011 finalist for the Pulitzer Prize, and his first book, *Lawrence Booth's Book of Visions* (Yale, 2001), was selected by W.S. Merwin for the Yale Younger Poets award.

DAVID MOOLTEN is the author of three books of poetry: *Plums & Ashes* (Northeastern, 1994), which won the Samuel French Morse Poetry Prize; *Especially Then* (David Robert, 2005) and *Primitive Mood* (Truman State, 2009), which won the T.S. Eliot Prize. He lives in Philadelphia.

AMANDA MOORE's debut collection of poetry, *Requeening* (Ecco, 2021), was selected for the 2020 National Poetry Series by Ocean Vuong. She is a high school English teacher and lives by the beach in the Outer Sunset neighborhood of San Francisco with her husband and daughter.

JESSE NATHAN was raised in Berkeley and south-central Kansas. He teaches literature at UC Berkeley and was a founding editor of the McSweeney's Poetry Series. His first collection, *Eggtooth* (Unbound Edition), will be published in September.

TANYA OLSON lives in Silver Spring, MD, and is a senior lecturer in English at the University of Maryland, Baltimore County. She is the author of *Boyishly* (YesYes, 2013), winner of a 2014 American Book Award, and *Stay* (YesYes, 2019). She has received the Discovery/Boston Review prize and was named a 2011 Lambda Fellow by the Lambda Literary Foundation. Her poem "54 Prince" was chosen for inclusion in *Best American Poetry 2015* (Scribner) by Sherman Alexie.

ROWAN RICARDO PHILLIPS has received a Guggenheim fellowship, a Whiting Award, two PEN awards and the Anisfield-Wolf Book Prize, as well as a finalist for the National Book Award and *The Los Angeles Times* Book Prize. He is the poetry editor of *The New Republic*. His most recent of his three books is *Living Weapon* (FSG, 2020).

FABIO PUSTERLA was born in Mendrisio, Switzerland, in 1957. He is a prolific poet, essayist and translator, most notably of the work of Philippe Jaccottet. His honors include the Swiss Schiller Prize, the Gottfried Keller-Preis and the Premio Napoli for lifetime achievement.

JESSA QUEYROUZE lives in southern Louisiana. She was born in New Orleans and received a degree in English and creative writing from Louisiana State University.

LANDEN RASZICK is a poet and musician from south Florida. He recently earned his MFA in poetry from the Writing Seminars at Johns Hopkins University. His poems have appeared in *Book of Matches*, *The American Journal of Poetry* and *The Rush*. He lives in Baltimore.

WILL SCHUTT is the author of *Westerly* (Yale, 2013), winner of the Yale Series of Younger Poets Prize, and translator of *My Life, I Lapped It Up: Selected Poems of Edoardo Sanguineti* (Oberlin, 2018) and *Brief Homage to Pluto and Other Poems* by Fabio Pusterla (Princeton, 2023), among other works from Italian.

JULIE SHEEHAN's three poetry collections are *Thaw* (Fordham, 2001), *Orient Point* (W.W. Norton, 2007) and *Bar Book* (W.W. Norton, 2010). A Whiting Writers' Award winner, Sheehan's work appeared in *The Best American Poetry 2005* (Scribner). She teaches in the creative writing program at Stony Brook University.

SARA MOORE WAGNER is the winner of the 2021 Cider Press Review Editors Prize for her book *Swan Wife* (2022) and the 2020 Driftwood Press Manuscript Prize for *Hillbilly Madonna* (2022). She is the author of two chapbooks, *Hooked Through* (Five Oaks, 2017) and *Tumbling After* (Red Bird, 2022). Wagner is a 2022 Ohio Arts Council Individual Excellence Award recipient, a 2021 National Poetry Series Finalist and the recipient of a 2019 Sustainable Arts Foundation award.

TIPHANIE YANIQUE's poetry collection, *Wife* (Tree, 2015), won the Bocas Prize in Caribbean poetry and the United Kingdom's Forward/Felix Dennis Prize for a First Collection. In 2010, she was named a "5 Under 35" honoree by the National Book Foundation and is a winner of a Boston Review Prize in Fiction, a Rona Jaffe Foundation Writers Award, a Pushcart Prize, a Fulbright Scholarship and an Academy of American Poets Prize. Born in Saint Thomas, U.S. Virgin Islands, she teaches creative writing at Emory University and lives in New York.

FELICIA ZAMORA is the author of six books of poetry, including *Body of Render* (Red Hen, 2020), a Benjamin Saltman Award winner; *I Always Carry My Bones* (U. of Iowa, 2021), winner of the 2020 Iowa Poetry Prize and the 2022 Ohioana Book Award in Poetry; and *Quotient* (Tinderbox, 2022). She won the 2020 C.P. Cavafy Prize from Poetry International, the 2022 Loraine Williams Poetry Prize from The Georgia Review, the Tomaž Šalamun Prize and a 2022 Ohio Arts Council Individual Excellence Award. She is an assistant professor of poetry at the University of Cincinnati and associate poetry editor for the *Colorado Review*.

MARIA ZOCCOLA's first book of poems, *Helen of Troy, 1993*, is forthcoming from Scribner in 2025. She has writing degrees from Emory University and Falmouth University.

Donations

FRIEND—$30 or more; listed for one issue, with a two-issue subscription.
    Anonymous (8)
    Anna Hyer
    Jason Miller
    Beth Vanderkin

ASSOCIATE—$100 or more; listed for two issues, with a four-issue subscription.
    Anonymous (3)

PATRON—$500 or more; listed for three issues, with a ten-issue subscription.

SPONSOR—$1,000 or more; listed for four issues, with a lifetime subscription.

BENEFACTOR—$3,000 or more; listed for five issues, with two lifetime subscriptions.

An independent nonprofit magazine, not affiliated with or supported by any institution, *Smartish Pace* needs the support of individual readers. Your donation is tax deductible to the fullest extent of the law and may be made at smartishpace.com or by mailing a check payable to *"Smartish Pace"* to: Smartish Pace, P.O. Box 22161, Baltimore, MD 21203. Smartish Pace, Inc. is a 501(c)3 nonprofit organization. The editors thank you for your support.

www.ingramcontent.com/pod-product-compliance
Lightning Source LLC
Chambersburg PA
CBHW032038040426
42449CB00007B/941